DONALD BARTHELME

A Study of the Short Fiction

Also available in Twayne's Studies in Short Fiction Series

Twayne's Studies in Short Fiction

Gordon Weaver, General Editor
Oklahoma State University

DONALD BARTHELME
Photograph by Jerry Bauer.

DONALD BARTHELME

A Study of the Short Fiction

Barbara L. Roe
Heritage Hall, Oklahoma City

TWAYNE PUBLISHERS • NEW YORK
Maxwell Macmillan Canada • Toronto
Maxwell Macmillan International • New York Oxford Singapore Sydney

Twayne's Studies in Short Fiction Series, No. 32

Copyright © 1992 by Twayne Publishers.

Twayne Publishers
Macmillan Publishing Company
866 Third Avenue
New York, NY 10022

Maxwell Macmillan Canada, Inc.
1200 Eglinton Avenue East
Suite 200
Don Mills, Ontario M3C 3N1

Macmillan Publishing Company is part of the Maxwell Communication Group of Companies.

Library of Congress Cataloging-in-Publication Data
Roe, Barbara L.
    Donald Barthelme : a study of the short fiction / Barbara L. Roe.
        p.   cm. — (Twayne's studies in short fiction series ; no. 32)
    Includes bibliographical references and index.
    ISBN 0-8057-8338-5 (alk. paper)
    1. Barthelme, Donald—Criticism and interpretation.   2. Short
story.   I. Title.   II. Series: Twayne's studies in short fiction;
no. 32.
PS3552.A76Z84   1992
813'.54—dc20   91-32992
                                                                            CIP

10 9 8 7 6 5 4 3 2 1

Printed in the United States of America.

To Tommy, Tyler, and Todd

Contents

Preface

Less than a decade after his *Come Back, Dr. Caligari* (1964) sidled up, thin and cartoonish, next to John Barth's tomes, Donald Barthelme ranked among America's most exciting, if controversial, short fiction writers. At the *New Yorker* offices, Roger Angell, his editor, witnessed this impact in the shift from "imitations of Salinger to imitations of Barthelme" that flooded the magazine.[1] On university campuses, creative writing classes burgeoned with inspired novices trying to duplicate his eccentricities. In 1973, the same year Charles Newman proclaimed Barthelme "the most imitated writer in [America] today,"[2] some brazen rival even managed to publish several forgeries before Barthelme exposed the charade. Capitalizing on Barthelme's reputation as a Robin Hood of the "trash phenomenon,"[3] Richard Lingeman parodied the disclaimer in a warning against the tainted spoils of literary crime: "Steal My Name and You Got Trash."[4] Finally, in 1976, the *New York Times Magazine* challenged imitators to vie legitimately by finishing a story begun by Barthelme. The task, several thousand discovered, was not as easy as it looked.

Paradoxically, Barthelme contenders were trying to imitate a style at first notorious for its surprises: fragmented texts with lists, headlines, typographical play, collage pasteups, numbered sentences, one long (endless) sentence, caricatures, mixed idioms. Working within a genre already issued its last rites, Barthelme seemed obsessed with crusading for "the new."[5] During the last decade of his life, his method became more predictable but also "more austere."[6] Often, he honed speech into pure dialogues—"bone bubbles" scored for discreet duets. In these fleeting exchanges, rude, rubbery words bump against delicate, lacy ones—like "U-joints in the vichyssoise"[7]—but their swelling nuances intimate symphonies of meaning. From the voices rise slang, argot, aphorism, hype, ballyhoo, and lyric—all finely tuned to Barthelme's keen ear. Readers, however, must ultimately conduct this welter, and some refuse the master's baton.

Historically, Barthelme's work has divided critics as well as popular audiences. Even while praising his inventive genius and brilliant lines, a number have doubted Barthelme's professed moral intent. They complain particularly that the absence of traditional short story structure—the precise maps of deed and thought—in his work alienates art from life, since Barthelme's speakers seem to float through contrived fantasies rather than beat the pavement of "real" landscapes. Others worry that the archly ironic tones and poses sell out human emotions. Some say the stories are pointlessly obscure. The *New Yorker* pieces "used to annoy and scare readers," recalls Roger Angell. "A lot deeply disliked them, mostly people without much humor." On a popular level, critic Richard Schickel tried to close this gap between idolatry and suspicion shortly after reviews of *City Life* (1970) ushered Barthelme into the literary spotlight's full glare. Imitating the question-answer format of several Barthelme stories, Schickel revealed associates' insights into Barthelme's life and work—how novelty jousts with boredom, how despair rivals achievement, how irony survives world error.[8] Though more comprehensive analyses have long since dated this "interview," the article is still a good place for uninitiated readers to shore themselves against wanton skepticism.

As Roger Angell implied, the first hook that snags readers is Barthelme's humor. His stories are often hilarious. Yet colleagues insist that, despite the jokes, Barthelme was a deeply serious intellect and an exacting artist. Though he abandoned Catholicism in youth, he did not abandon faith: faith in mankind's creative wellsprings rather than in some grand cosmic design. He coveted the mysteries of words— their "halos, patinas, overhangs, echoes"[9]—but he despised their parade in gaudy ensembles. According to John Barth, this "thinking man's—and woman's—Minimalist" typically kept language on a "rhetorical short leash."[10] Olive Hershey recalls how Barthelme inspired this passion for "discipline" and "restraint" in his students, too: "The best thing I learned from Barthelme is to cut my work in half. Literally. Half the words, half the adjectives, half the descriptive passages. I watched him edit my manuscript for *Truck Dance*. The scene was this. We're sitting at my dining room table. He's got a pencil. I'm seated next to him. He takes the pencil and starting at the top of the page draws a strong black line through every line on the page. Then he looks over at me. 'Okay?' he says. 'Okay,' I say. 'Good woman,' he says."[11] Humor and good will softened the perfectionist's edges.

So Barthelme was not being flip or coy or frivolous when he wrote his spare fiction. In fact, says Harrison Starr, he was "'an extraordinarily gentle and ethical man' with 'a very naked eye for pain'" (quoted in Schickel, 44). Because he wanted readers to "feel" rather than "know" his visions, however, Barthelme sometimes despaired if he could not intellectualize on a lofty, artistic plane the deeper insights of his soul. "Ideally," he wrote, a story's revelations "should frighten your shoes" (*N*, 47). He wanted his fiction to register emotion despite the austere structures of his language, a difficult compromise to achieve, particularly in his early work.[12] Still, his successes were poignant, startling. In the dialogue "Great Days," for instance, rage chokes on disappointment as one voice articulates youth's foolish acts of energy and hope: "Tied flares to my extremities and wound candy canes into my lustrous, abundant hair. Getting ready for the great day" (*F*, 232). But the gray dusk of lost love, lost prospects later gathers in a gloomy refrain: "He told me terrible things in the evening of that day as we sat side by side waiting for the rain to wash the watercolors from his watercolor paper. Waiting for the rain to wash the paper clean, quite clean" (*F*, 236; variation, 242–43). As Barth stresses, moreover, the most Spartan line is sometimes the most wrenching: "At his tersest, with a single comma he can constrict your heart: 'I visited the child's nursery school, once'" (1989, 9).

In the conventional sense, Barthelme did not write "short stories." He even suggested that *prose poems* or *contes* better fit the style and mythic cloth of his lean, dense works. Without the aid of such explicit parameters as plot, character, and obvious theme, how do we read his short fiction? There is no one way. In fact, mused Roger Angell, a story's allusive possibilities are often so thick that even an urbane *New Yorker* audience can only speculate on Barthelme's intentions. Critical to the fiction's structures, however, are contemporary views of mankind's status in an indeterminate world. Modern theories of relativity conceive of space "not as one-sided or linear—as in the Renaissance idea of perspective—but as many-sided and virtually inexhaustible in its potentiality for relationships, none of which are mutually exclusive."[13] Similarly, time is not just a linear framework for the history of mankind, or even for the chronological development of an individual's life, as in the bildungsroman. It also includes the overlapping perspectives of each person's memory, dream, and imagination. In addition, multimedia's data overload renders life's "facts" unintelligible from any one viewpoint. Complicated by mechanical warps—instant replays, slow-motion takes, the nightly news montage, the staggering time lag between a star's implosion and its recognition by observers on earth—what "facts" are communicated seem unmanageable, unreal.

Though such views belie fiction's dated rubric for truth, Barthelme turns indeterminacy to the advantage of his audience and his art.

It is illuminating, if not conclusive, therefore, to read his work as both comment on and instance of the generic evolution spurred by world changes, particularly the ferment of the 1960s, when Barthelme's short fiction first gained national attention. Hence, this study suggests beginning where Barthelme began—with the double vision of parody and myth. Though the preface to *Guilty Pleasures* apologizes for his merry indulgence in parody and bills that volume's pieces as "nonfiction," critics generally agree that this disclaimer is moot. After all, most of his *New Yorker* pieces, with their notorious mocking poses, subsequently appear in Barthelme's short fiction books. To compromise these opposing perspectives, Robert Scholes's distinction of parody as a "surgical response" to exhausted literary forms, rather than distortion of a specific work, is useful.[14] Thus, the critical analyses in Part 1 first consider pieces that overturn the writer's depleted legacy by playing against the reader's conditioned expectations. Interestingly, Barthelme's techniques for contemporizing myth—engaging the reader's familiarity with heroic tales and figures—work on much the same principle as the parodies. But the myths also glow with the creative fires that illuminate Barthelme's faith in ordinary life's mysteries—almost an obsession in the later work. Because the stories loosely embraced by these two structures flaunt their comic effects, they are among the most inviting to read and, again, an excellent place to start.

The next two parts analyze more demanding and controversial works. Borrowing techniques from related arts, Barthelme explored ways to suggest the contemporary world's inexhaustible perspectives. In these aural and visual complexes, a spatially designed text displaces linear plot, an ahistorical presence supersedes character, and a collage format fragments narrative viewpoint. The resulting absences—essential to the fiction's intrigue—paradoxically provoke the reader's need for meaningful systems while they simultaneously encourage "assent" to disorder.[15] The ethic of thus involving the audience in art's dilemmas and joys is the focus of the third section's analyses—critiques that scrutinize the moral undertow of surface complexities, even where parody and myth remain quite busy.

Like the titles *Sixty Stories* and *Forty Stories*, these three groupings are conveniences, not strict orders. Taken with the autobiographical and critical excerpts that follow, however, they locate Barthelme's work in the mainstream of postmodern short fiction. To facilitate reference,

I cite Barthelme's two large collections whenever possible, noting any pertinent changes from originally published texts.

The purpose of this book is, above all, to share the intellectual and spiritual excitement of reading Barthelme's short fiction. Though I may not rally converts from the skeptics' camp, it will be clear where I have pitched my own tent. For the opportunity to write this study, I am indebted to several people: Professor Robert Murray Davis, a persistent mentor, for recommending me to the project; editors Gordon Weaver of Oklahoma State University and Liz Fowler of Twayne Publishers for seasoned advice and uncommon humanity; and especially Donald Barthelme for his generous gifts of time and art. In addition, Roger Angell, Olive Hershey, Jose Arroyo at Putnam's, and Christina West and Clare Ruggles at the University of Houston Creative Writing Program deserve special mention for many kindnesses. I also thank other Barthelme enthusiasts for sharing their insights, Heritage Hall for a brief study-leave, and dear friends for jolly support. My deepest gratitude, however, is to the wise love of my family. Circling my soul, they chant their faith in silence.

Notes

1. Roger Angell, telephone interview, 14 April 1989; hereafter cited in the text.
2. Charles Newman, "The Uses and Abuses of Death: A Little Rumble through the Remnants of Literary Culture," *TriQuarterly* 26 (Winter 1973): 38.
3. This notoriety arose from a narrative comment in *Snow White* (New York: Atheneum, 1967), 98.
4. Richard Lingeman, "Steal My Name and You Got Trash," *New York Times Book Review*, 3 February 1974, 39.
5. "The Literature of Exhaustion," *Atlantic Monthly*, August 1967, 29–34, John Barth's discussion of the novel's weary conventions and new possibilities, is pertinent for short fiction, too.
6. Interview with author, 19 August 1988, in Houston, Texas; unless otherwise noted, all further background data and authorial comments are based on this interview.
7. *Forty Stories* (New York: G. P. Putnam's Sons, 1987), 236; hereafter cited in the text as *F*.
8. Richard Schickel, "Freaked Out on Barthelme," *New York Times Magazine*, 16 August 1970, 14–15, 42; hereafter cited in the text.
9. "Not-Knowing," in *Voicelust*, ed. Allen Wier and Don Hendrie, Jr.

(Lincoln: University of Nebraska Press, 1985), 47; hereafter cited in the text as *N*.

10. John Barth, "Thinking Man's Minimalist: Honoring Barthelme," *New York Times Book Review*, 3 September 1989, 9; hereafter cited in the text.

11. Olive Hershey, letter to author, 19 May 1989.

12. Though no bold changes separate Barthelme's "early" and "later" work, this study's analyses support several stylistic and thematic currents in roughly the first and last decades' fiction.

13. Sharon Spencer, *Space, Time, and Structure in the Modern Novel* (New York: New York University Press, 1971), xvii–xviii; for further discussion, see Mas'ud Zavarzadeh, *The Mythopoeic Reality: The Postwar American Nonfiction Novel* (Urbana: University of Illinois Press, 1976), 3–32.

14. Robert Scholes, "Metafiction," *Iowa Review* 1 (Fall 1970): 103.

15. "Assent" is virtually the sovereign domain of Alan Wilde; see "Barthelme Unfair to Kierkegaard," *Horizons of Assent: Modernism, Postmodernism, and the Ironic Imagination* (Baltimore: Johns Hopkins University Press, 1981), 183–188.

Acknowledgments

Permission to reprint excerpts from the following previously published material is gratefully acknowledged:

"The Art of Fiction LXVI," by J. D. O'Hara, in the *Paris Review* 80 (Summer 1981): 181–210, by permission of the authors and the *Paris Review*. © 1981 by the *Paris Review*.

"Donald Barthelme," by Jerome Klinkowitz, in *The New Fiction: Interviews with Innovative American Writers*, ed. Joe David Bellamy, by permission of the University of Illinois Press. © 1974 by the Board of Trustees of the University of Illinois.

Donald Barthelme, by Maurice Couturier and Régis Durand, by permission of Methuen and Co., New York and London. © 1982 by Maurice Couturier and Régis Durand.

"Failed Artists in Donald Barthelme's *Sixty Stories*," by Lee Upton, *Critique* 26 (Fall 1984): 11–17. Reprinted by permission of the Helen Dwight Reid Educational Foundation. Published by Heldref Publications, 4000 Albemarle St., N.W., Washington, D.C. 20016. © 1984 by the Helen Dwight Reid Educational Foundation.

Forty Stories, by Donald Barthelme, by permission of the Putnam Publishing Group. © 1987 by Donald Barthelme.

"An Interview with Donald Barthelme," by Larry McCaffery, in *Anything Can Happen: Interviews with Contemporary American Novelists*, ed. Tom LeClair and Larry McCaffery, by permission of the University of Illinois Press. © 1983 by the Board of Trustees of the University of Illinois.

The Metafictional Muse: The Works of Robert Coover, Donald Barthelme, and William H. Gass, by Larry McCaffery, by permission of the University of Pittsburgh Press. © 1982 by University of Pittsburgh Press.

Middle Grounds: Studies in Contemporary American Fiction, by Alan Wilde, by permission of the University of Pennsylvania Press. © 1987 by University of Pennsylvania Press.

"Not-Knowing," by Donald Barthelme, in *Voicelust*, ed. Allen Wier

Acknowledgments

and Don Hendrie, Jr., by permission of Donald Barthelme. © 1985 by
Donald Barthelme.

Overnight to Many Distant Cities, by Donald Barthelme, by permission
of the Putnam Publishing Group. © 1983 by Donald Barthelme.

Sixty Stories, by Donald Barthelme, by permission of Wylie, Aitken
and Stone, Inc. © 1981 by Donald Barthelme.

Part 1

THE SHORT FICTION

A Game of Mixed Doubles

"I'm fated to deal in mixtures, slumgullions," Barthelme confessed. "As soon as I hear a proposition I immediately consider its opposite." This "double-minded man,"[1] who migrated seasonally between apartments near sprawling Houston boulevards and the congested hubs of lower Manhattan, sprang from a richly varied heritage that traverses American culture. His great-grandfather ran a bar in Brooklyn; his paternal grandfather ran bases for a semiprofessional ball team and finally skipped to Galveston to develop a lumber business. Attending the University of Pennsylvania, Barthelme's parents nurtured more ethereal interests: his mother, English; his father, architecture. But even these Olympian creatures were smitten with double vision and occasionally performed antics on sublime terrain. Barthelme's fate was eventually dealt by gods who laughed over the *New Yorker* and tossed *A Subtreasury of American Humor* amid mythology and architectural books on the family coffee table. Slamming a shin into the furniture, the youth might have tumbled with S. J. Perelman or lurched headlong into E. B. White's "Dusk in Fierce Pajamas."[2] In the thirties, moreover, the family and its home were "something of an anomaly. . . . on the Texas prairie."[3] Created from his father's infatuation with Mies modernism, the Barthelme homestead was a weekend sightseer's curiosity. Sundays, Barthelme recalled, the whole family—the architect, the English major, the gifted children—used to rise from dinner, "if enough cars had parked, and run out in front of the house in a sort of chorus line, doing high kicks" (Klinkowitz 1974, 47). The gods were riotous folk.

From low comedy to lofty art, contrary influences initially encouraged Barthelme's interest in two equally diverse literary forms: parody and myth. As a novice writer for the Lamar High School literary magazine and newspaper, Barthelme began to explore his craft with delightfully comic distortions of his predecessors. "Rover Boys' Retrogression," published in *Sequoyah 1948–49*, for instance, is the "antithesis" of *Pilgrim's Progress* in both theme and form. The mock pilgrimage in Barthelme's version of Bunyan's allegory follows the misadventures of Half-Asleep and Not-Quite-Awake through the hills and valleys of adolescence to the boys' ultimate goal: expulsion from the Houston Independent School District at the Banks of the River of Respect Due. Despite the amateurish content of this lampoon, Barthelme showed an incisive grasp of parody's structure and purpose. In the preface to his mock allegory, he includes the definition to which he commits his text: "A parody, to be completely effective *as a parody*, must be a complete reversal of attitude, set in the form of the work being parodied" (4). Though the narrow scope of the definition binds the accompanying text to a standard form—parody of a specific work, its conventions, or the affectations of its author—it is nevertheless keyed to a serious game of reversed intentions popular with Barthelme and other innovative fiction writers little more than a decade later.

By the mid-1960s Barthelme's definition had broadened to allow him to shadowbox a "whole class of things."[4] In a somewhat cavalier introduction to *Guilty Pleasures*, Barthelme wrote that for a parody to be effective, "A minimum demand is that what is parodied be widely successful—a tulip craze of some sort."[5] In the 1960s his fancy targeted fashionable social themes—the absurdity of existence, the uncertainty of self, the fear of science, the fear of one's fellow man—and struck repeatedly on the popular literary theme of the times, the outmoded conventions perpetuated by "the Novelist," a nineteenth-century know-it-all expected to deliver life's crises and solutions within the tidy confines of a fictional microcosm.

Under this broader definition of parody, the first several pieces critiqued here play upon the relentless absurdity of contemporary life that the artist struggles to match or contain. The method of these stories is essentially a game played in reverse of the "ordinary rules," a sort of inverse form of mimesis: instead of representing an ideal order out of chaos, it confuses at every point what the reader (Player 2) expects of the writer (Player 1) and of literary convention. Applied to fiction's ordinary rules, the game in reverse is the construction of a mock narrative enacted by a masque of faceless caricatures:

> Rule 1. Unobstructed routes are not permitted. As Player 1 lures his opponent from Start to Finish, the paths of plot must be blocked at every turn with lists, questionnaires, blank pages, meandering digressions, sloughs of clichés, or narratives stalled by anticlimax.
> Rule 2. Members of the masque must disguise their humanity in

two-dimensional roles, since Player 2 will covet any character with a credible identity.

Rule 3. Throwing Doubles. Player 1 may dissemble himself, his characters, his audience, his publisher; he may hold mirrors to fictions and mirrors to mirrors.

Rule 4. End of Play. If at any time Player 1 does not successfully check his opponent's expectations, he forfeits the game—unless, of course, he changes the rules.

One consequence of these mixed doubles is that fiction "unmask[s] its own fictionality."[6] Heroic pilgrimage therefore digresses into aimless yo-yoing; credibility of character collapses in comic-strip names; and preoccupation with order and symbol becomes an obsessive pursuit of meaning in repetition.

Despite the caprice of its method, this type of parody serves a purpose both unique and serious: it is the one literary mode that "fuses creation with critique."[7] Critics, in fact, abound in Barthelme's stories. Characters criticize each other, criticize their creator, criticize the tales in which they find themselves. The narrators of "The Balloon" and "This Newspaper Here" parry threats and suspicion; the writers in "The Dolt" and "Florence Green Is 81" are accused of lacking talent; the narrator of "See the Moon?" confesses to his reader, "I know you think I'm wasting my time. You've made that perfectly clear. . . . My methods may seem a touch irregular."[8] Caught, however unwillingly, in these regressions of doubling plots and roles, the reader is finally jarred from his fatuous acceptance of things as they are or things as they appear. Yet even as he questions the status of fiction, his role as a critic, like all other roles within or outside the parody, is only tenuous. The legitimacy of his findings is never affirmed, the ironies never stable, as they are in a standard parody such as "Rover Boys' Retrogression."

Only "Eugénie Grandet" (originally cast as "nonfiction" but reprinted in *Sixty Stories*) is a conventional parody that mocks a specific text. "Eugénie Grandet," however, is yet another instance of Barthelme's double vision, for, unlike the other parodies, it shares a collage format with the more inventive fictions discussed in the next section. Similarly, "A Shower of Gold," presented as a bridge between parody and myth, fires in two directions at once: it first mocks the demoralized artist Peterson but then transforms him into a hero of dubious parentage who claims the high ground of Olympia.

Long an admirer of Joseph Campbell's *The Hero with a Thousand Faces*,[9] Barthelme said that tapping old myths' "provocative power" intrigued him. This ambitious project inspired three novel-length works—*Snow White* (1967), *The Dead Father* (1975), and *The King* (1990)—and a host of "heroic" sketches. Like the parodies, both the novels and the smaller studies of legendary figures engage readers' familiarity with timeworn tales yet comically upend their mythic doubles. For instance, though Greek gods were notorious for harboring petty grievances and frequently meddled in mortals' affairs, power was their birthright. No one questioned their deed to the heavens. But Barthelme's bold creatures—Daumier, Paul Klee, Mad Moll—typically dwell with or near mankind and enjoy only brief heavenly tours. Perhaps their sole relative among the deities of yore is the craftsman Hephaestus, the sweaty, limping god of the forge, whose destiny of enduring tough love is ordinary fare in Barthelme's fiction. Abhorring her son's ugliness, mother Hera cast the infant Hephaestus from the heavens into an earthly sea; his desirable wife Aphrodite scandalized him with her indiscretions; and temperamental father Zeus crippled his son by dashing Hephaestus, once more, to the earth. Barthelme's characters repeatedly suffer variations on this immortal's inevitable abuses. Notably, women scorn men yet entice their prey with luscious dainties. The collision of Balloon Man and Pin Lady in a "great hug," for instance, is fated: "It's in the cards, in the stars, in the entrails of sacred animals. . . . Their stances are semiantireprophetical" (*SS*, 314–15). Moreover, unless offspring inherit the mother's malice, fathers wound their sons (though the *Dead* Father drags around a mechanical leg and lusts unsuccessfully after mortal nymphs). As Barthelme's "double-minded" perspective regenerates myth, the lives of artists and common folk are seldom removed from his heroes' misadventures.

Merrily hop-shuffling through "mixtures, slumgullions," Barthelme's irreverent personae invite readers to join them in a chorus of high kicks. The bold ones, faithful as lemmings, eagerly lock arms. Yet "games," muses a vacuous Barthelme character, "are the enemies of beauty, truth, and sleep" (*GP*, 134), and they can mesmerize the masses with wayward diversions. Alluding to an observation by American psychologist Gregory Bateson, Barthelme explains that humor may be a "great alternative to psychosis . . . . a kind of necessary defense mechanism," but it is a spurious alternative for art.[10] Thus, while Barthelme's parodies comically mime stilted conventions, they often play with myth upon artistic alternatives and thematically, at least, inspire the technical virtuosity and moral tones of stories like those in *Overnight to Many Distant Cities*. Eventually, fierce of purpose, hale of heart, Barthelme dismantles some of parody's detours. Replacing them with the doubles of myth and invention, he ensures art's persistent meditation on life.

The Parodies: Subversive Play
"The Dolt"

During the throes of generic shift, Barthelme suggested, the writer's predicament is similar to "having one's coat pulled, frequently by five people in six directions" (*GP*, prefatory comment). Hounded by his audience's "rage for final explanations,"[11] the author and his surrogates struggle to exorcise, as John Barth said, the specter of the "ditto necessary story."[12] One response is denial that the haunt is theirs. The schizophrenic persona in "Florence Green Is 81," for instance, describes himself as a "brilliant" young man, a "weightlifter and poet,"[13] but ultimately blunders into revealing that the dull, foolish Baskerville whom he has disparaged throughout the story is really his rebuffed alter ego. In "The Dolt," however, the witless artist never escapes his fate.

A prototype for all the "unspeakable practices, unnatural acts" suffered by Barthelme's artists, "The Dolt" first exposes Edgar as he prepares to take the National Writers' Examination, "black with fear" (*SS*, 92) that he will fail it for the third time. Studying the rules, a book of questions similar to the actual questions on the examination, Edgar hopes this time to earn a certificate that will merit his work's publication in reputable journals and win him a bit of faith from his disdainful wife, Barbara. Trying as much to allay his fears as to reassure his spouse, Edgar ironically boasts that while the written test is, to be sure, a source of worry, he can pass the oral part of the examination with ease. He then attempts to bait his wife and secure her encouragement by showing his skill at playing the game in reverse, giving Barbara a list of answers and challenging her to give him the right questions. But she will not pamper his ego. "Barb," as he calls her, is "sexually attractive . . . but also deeply mean" (*SS*, 92); given the answer *Julia Ward Howe*, she levels Edgar by responding with the correct question.

The thrust of this self-parody appears in the second half of "The Dolt," when Barthelme assumes the persona of the paranoiac writer and constructs a fiction within the parody—the story that Edgar has prepared for the written portion of his examination. Barbara's interest is piqued. Though the story has no title, its beginning shows promise: a good plot moved by heroism in battle, framed by the proverbial lovers' triangle, and complicated by innocence wronged, by the vengeful manipulations of a jealous husband against chaste lovers. A grand hierarchy of values—chastity, fidelity, heroism—is threatened with ruin. But Edgar's reading is brief, little more than an outline of the potential story. In addition, the writing is marred by convoluted sentences, shifts in verb tense, an archaic style, and a peculiar mixture of historical "facts" with fiction. Edgar's doom is sealed, however, when he must confess that his story has no middle and only an oblique denouement.

The crux of the writer's problem, this self-parody reveals, is that nothing in his life supports any system of value represented in the writing models Edgar has studied. Barbara, a former hooker, hardly symbolizes chastity. Her suggestion for his story's middle is a jaded anecdote about an illicit love affair and a woman who spontaneously aborts in Chicago. Edgar's silent, staring daughter Rose seems dear, yet swathed in a terry-cloth robe, she menaces like a diminutive boxer, and her mien belies the fragility of her name. Edgar's imagination fails entirely, though, when into the room slinks his eight-foot, "son manqué" (a startling parody of the eight-foot priest/soldier/lover in Edgar's story). The youth is bedecked with a "serape woven out of two hundred transistor radios, all turned on and tuned to different stations. Just by looking at him you could hear Portland and Nogales, Mexico" (*SS*, 96).

As Edgar withdraws in despair, a first-person, very tansparent persona steps from the parody to lament the aspiring writer's paralysis: "I sympathize. I myself have these problems. Endings are elusive, middles are nowhere to be found, but worst of all is to begin, to begin, to begin" (*SS*, 96).

"The Balloon"

Reversing his aim, Barthelme also parodies contemporary audiences, suspicious or fearful of experimental art. Just as the writer's personae are alternately depicted as hostile and sympathetic in "Florence Green" and "The Dolt," audience reaction to anomaly may vary from the pistol-whipping detective's malevolence in "This Newspaper Here" to the inquisitors' naïveté in "The Great Hug" and "The Balloon." In the latter, reaction creates a dot-to-dot pattern, rather than a linear story, as a first-person narrator zigzags from one voice to another, logging responses to his enigmatic objet trouvé. *What* these voices say should elicit as much scrutiny as the object that provokes them to speak.

In conspiracy with the night, the narrator/artist mysteriously releases a shape-shifting balloon to expand over much of Manhattan. The next day, a few puzzled New Yorkers stroll the landscape of its upper surfaces, bounce on it, write messages, or hang "green and blue paper lanterns from the warm gray underside" (*SS*, 54). Others try to label it, to use jargon's blanketing effect to mitigate confusion or anxiety:

"monstrous pourings"

"harp"

XXXXXXX "certain contrasts with darker portions"
   "inner joy"
"large, square corners"
"conservative eclecticism that has so far governed
 modern balloon design"
 :::::::: "abnormal vigor"
"warm, soft lazy passages"
"Has unity been sacrificed for a sprawling quality?"
 "Quelle catastrophe!"
  "munching"

(*SS*, 56–57)

But the balloon, which continues to expand and change shape long after the artist has created it, defies all efforts to formulate its meaning with empty phrases. The narrator/artist cautions that "we have learned not to insist on meanings, and they are rarely even looked for now, except in cases involving the simplest, safest phenomena" (*SS*, 54). Instead, the balloon inspires multiple random and contradictory perspectives. Its appeal, the New Yorkers suggest, is that it is "not limited, or defined" (*SS*, 57). For many citizens—particularly uninhibited children who abandon language for joyful leaps upon the undulating surfaces—the balloon is a source of imaginative release from "rigidly patterned" lives and from the city's labyrinth, a "grid of precise, rectangular pathways" (*SS*, 57).

First-person narrative viewpoint similarly shifts. For the artistic "I," busy with the mechanics of hanging his exhibit, the balloon is a unique phenomenon, a professional triumph; his success, like that of Balloon Man in "The Great Hug," requires the perfect "gesture—the precise, reunpremeditated right move" (*SS*, 314). For the passionate "I" who removes the exhibit, however, the balloon is a "spontaneous autobiographical disclosure" (*SS*, 58), buoyed by poignant human emotions: longing for an absent lover, sadness, anger. ("Not every balloon," laments "The Great Hug" narrator, "can make you happy" [*SS*, 316]). Thus, over the course of the story, the balloon variously poses as object, landscape, and symbol—forms that language fails to define.

As this conclusion suggests, "The Balloon" not only parodies the audience's unsettled role, but also reveals two other concerns persistent in Barthelme's stories: the contamination of language (stamping the balloon with "LABORATORY TESTS PROVE" [*SS*, 55] would feign legitimacy and earn the object immediate social acceptance) and the ambiguous status of contemporary art. The labyrinthine prison of New York seems a contemporary American version of Joyce's Dublin, and the artist's creation, like that of Joyce, Yeats, or even Daedalus, appears to be the only means of escape. Unlike the modernist writers (and a few characters), however, Barthelme does not retreat in exile to a refuge among darkened battlements, nor is his art the aesthetically scoured and impersonal work of some predecessors. Rather than soar above the maze on Icarian wings, the balloon artist, for instance, releases his creation just above the city and then remains with his audience in the labyrinth to share their responses as they ponder the object. Moreover, instead of rising beyond the city, the balloon waltzes in the buildings' embrace. Gently pressing the skyscrapers, its protean surfaces extend and continuously modify the landscape: "Each intersection was crucial, meeting of balloon and building, meeting of balloon and man, meeting of balloon and balloon" (*SS*, 57). Most importantly, though, while the balloon remains within the bounds of the city, it encourages the liberating play of imagination—a strategy also gamefully exploited in "The Great Hug" by a motley cast of little blimps (the Balloon of Ora Pro Nobis; the Balloon of Grace Under Pressure, Do Not Pierce or Incinerate; the Rune Balloon [*SS*, 314–15]) and Pin Lady's counteragents (the Pin of I Violently Desire, the Pin of Crossed Fingers Behind My Back, the Pin of No More [*SS*, 315]).

The metaphor for Barthelme's art, therefore, is appropriately an exaggerated emblem of a child's fantasy for flight projected onto a toy loosely tethered to earth. Yet the "purpose" of *this* balloon is "not to amuse children" (*SS*, 55); neither is it intended to encourage the citylifers to raze or escape the labyrinth. What the contemporary artist's creation offers, finally, is a way of living with reality by assenting to art's possibilities. "The Balloon of Perhaps," says Balloon Man. "My best balloon" (*SS*, 316).

"The Glass Mountain"

In addition to altering the audience's habitual perception of the artist and itself, Barthelme's parodies may disrupt the expected order of narrative form and reduce archetypal figures to caricature. Opposing chronological sequence, Barthelme ends the narrative of "The Dolt" with "to begin, to begin, to begin." Conversely, he frustrates the comforting perspective of false beginnings by allowing "The Balloon" artist to obscure his creation's point of entry. Throughout "The Glass Mountain," however, Barthelme sustains reversals by encouraging his audience to bounce between a hypothetical narrative and twin mockeries.

The tale's framework transforms conventional fiction's linear sequence into a plodding yet playful scheme. One hundred consecutively numbered sentences vertically descend the page as a resourceful narrator, aided by a "plumber's friend" (*SS*, 178), scales the glistening mountain. Since the story begins with the narrator's precarious efforts, the reader expects a series of difficulties to follow and the story's action to climax when the hero triumphs. However, the plot labors as attention repeatedly shifts to the sights and sounds below: "28. In the streets were hundreds of young people shooting up in doorways . . ."; "30. The sidewalks were full of dogshit in brilliant colors, ocher, umber, Mars yellow, sienna, viridian, ivory black, rose madder" (*SS*, 179). At the base of the mountain, a crowd of thrillseekers cheers the hero on to failure: "11. 'Shithead'"; "12. 'Asshole'" (*SS*, 178).

From the first sentence—"1. I was trying to climb the glass mountain" (*SS*, 178)—the reader also expects rich symbols. After all, this is no weedy knoll. The hero, too, anticipates heavenly treasures: "a castle of pure gold"; "a beautiful enchanted symbol" (*SS*, 180). Unruffled by the crowd and an uncompromising eagle, he reviews by rote the "conventional means of attaining the castle" (*SS*, 181). Finally, he gains the slippery summit. Yet there at the quest's metaphorical climax, he discovers that the enchanted icon that he has sought for its revelations is just a comely princess. Like Barthelme's Snow White, who discovers that her suitor Paul is not a prince, but *"pure frog,"*[14] the narrator is disgusted with his prize. He flings the damsel over the edge to share the fate of the mountain's fallen knights and steeds. Though Hephaestus would have relished this ending, the hero's hopes plummet, like the princess and the plot.

Similar to "The Balloon," "The Glass Mountain" is quite busy with implications beyond the mock-narrative's antics. While the latter's public mercilessly brutalizes the story's quixotic protagonist, he himself errs by attempting to reaffirm the sacred ruins of another century's art right there between Thirteenth Street and Eighth Avenue. Barthelme's own insistence that "art is always a meditation upon external reality" (*N*, 49), not itself, exposes the mistake. First, so intent is the narrator upon his romantic quest that he tries to ignore his inevitable bonds to the phenomenological world: the city's crude particularity continually vies for his attention with the mountain's false enchantments and specious guides to their attainment (*A Dictionary of Literary Terms, The Yellow Fairy Book*). Second, he overlooks his artist's capacity to reveal the ordinary world's beauty—a mystery now far more powerful than sign or symbol. According to Wayne Stengel, "Only through the eyes of the thoroughly romantic narrator, and not through any vision of the people themselves, does the dog shit lining the streets acquire the rainbow of color of the artist's palette."[15]

The thematic and structural implications of "The Glass Mountain" for Barthelme's artistic experiments are apparent, as Stengel notes, in the ironic dismissals of "Nothing: A Preliminary Account" and of the portrait-with-questions "Concerning the Bodyguard." They are also dramatically manifested in the balloon tally of "The Great Hug," the breathless litany of "Sentence," and the purer linguistic play of "Bone Bubbles." Barthelme's discussion of "The Emerald," whose impotent witch, gem of an offspring, and coveted reliquary recall the trappings of "The Glass Mountain," clarifies the relationship among these stories. Comparing the world's disenchantment with symbols to the paucity of language, he suggested that the writer's true quest is, through words, to reinvest the world with magic (O'Hara, 207). Whereas "The Glass Mountain" and, to a greater degree, "The Emerald" muse upon this idea, "Bone Bubbles" indulges the effort to extremes. The textual words themselves are as ordinary as oil on a palette. But Barthelme said that their mixtures provide a mortar—a sort of "sand and concrete" of their own. Fastidiously interlocked, their combinations radiate mystery. Like the fictional balloon or the climber's rainbow visions, they may not declare their secrets all at once, but they focus Barthelme's art in "sharp particularity" (*N*, 47) upon the world's elusive beauties.

"Eugénie Grandet"

Unlike the preceding parodies, "Eugénie Grandet" is more interesting for its technical maneuvers—particularly its use of collage—than for its meditation on contemporary art. Still, the strategies of "Eugénie Grandet" and numerous other stories are directly related to the deflation of plot in "The Glass Mountain" and its ilk. A consequence of his "displacing the value of linear structure," explains Neil Schmitz, is that "Barthelme necessarily dislocates the centrality of characterization."[16] The compositions in *Come Back, Dr. Caligari*, for instance, feature sketchy caricatures of people disconnected, bored, identified only by the unimaginative lives that they create for themselves. Furthermore, that their identities can never be fixed or individuated is a source of paranoiac fear for such characters as Burligame in "Hiding Man." Shuttling over a grid of coordinates laid out in the horizontal and vertical rows of theater seats, Burligame tries to "plot" his own moves and considers with suspicion the mysterious intruder Bane-Hipkiss: "All of life is rooted in contradiction, movement in direction of self, two spaces, diagonally, argues hidden threat" (*CB*, 27).

But perhaps the stories that most effectively level the climactic contours of plot, particularly as those contours are shaped by a central character wrangling with a moral or social dilemma, are Barthelme's caricaturistic portrait studies ("Alice," "The Teachings of Don B.: A Yankee Way of Knowledge," "Eugénie Grandet").[17] Among such portraits, "Eugénie Grandet," a collage of narrative shards and mock illustrations, glorifies the parodic method, even as it bids farewell to this "disreputable activity" (*GP*, prefatory comment). On the most basic level, it conventionally subverts the plot, characters, manners, and values of Honoré de Balzac's bourgeoisie novel of the same name. On a more complex level, it extends the perimeters of play to parody book digests, epistolary forms, illustrated texts, and, again, the contemporary artist's creations. It is also the only intermedia composition reprinted in *Sixty Stories*.

The fragmented text of "Eugénie Grandet" humorously recalls melodramatic moments from the original story. In Balzac's version, after Eugénie's beloved cousin Charles Grandet is orphaned and left financially destitute, two subplots throttle forward. First, Eugénie discovers an unfinished letter that reveals that Charles is bidding farewell to his love Annette because he will be dishonored by his deceased father's debts. Though Eugénie is crushed by her discovery that she must abandon hope of having Charles for herself, she resolves, martyr-fashion, to give him all her money. Meanwhile, Eugénie's father plots a miser's vengeance; he hopes to avoid paying his brother's debts without incurring shame and, if possible, to turn a handy profit. Grandet's unscrupulous ploy is to stammer in the presence of his banker and notary until they are literally forced to put the words of his plan into his mouth. By feigning ignorance and a dull wit, he similarly gains the confidence of his adversaries. Throughout the novel, his every act is performed in the worship of Mammon. So consuming is his passion that even after his death, Eugénie remains emotionally impoverished.

Barthelme's version, on the other hand, opens with a deadpan summary of Balzac's novel from *The Thesaurus of Book Digests*. This insipid statement not only deflates Balzac's tragic tone, but also levels his grandiose design, reducing the writer's illusion of evil tyrannizing the world to cheap sleight-of-hand. It was all a trick, he implies. Then the doubling mechanism begins. Once more, Barthelme minimizes the original story, this time unraveling plot until just a few disparate threads, mere fragments of misinformation, remain, and the microcosmic unity of the novel is lost. While the reader can fill gaps in chronology by referring to the synopsis at the parody's outset, the characters themselves never imply the passing of time, since they do not mature beyond the limited impressions that they initially project. Instead, the original characters are glimpsed only through the inarticulate dialogue of a contemporary idiom (Eugénie on social repressions: "It's a whole . . . I guess atmosphere is the word . . . a tendency on the part of the society" [*SS*, 238]), and trivial concerns diminish worldly motives. Eugénie wants butter for her beloved Charles's eclair, but her father refuses her request. Eugénie's building resentment for her father—evoked chiefly by a paragraph in which "butter" is stamped out 87 times into rigid columns (an insulting mime of Grandet's stammering)—first prompts a lame attempt to put down her foot (stamp, stamp, stamp, stamp) and later compels her to kill him by giving her entire allowance to the church. Old Grandet suffers a "death by gasping" (*SS*, 244). Any potential for climactic action collapses in Eugénie's disproportionate anger, reduced in the butter episode to a childish tantrum.

Barthelme's parodic game is most engaging, however, when he in-

14

dulges his own "guilty pleasure," a penchant for "cutting up and pasting together pictures, a secret vice gone public" (*GP,* prefatory comment). This type of composition gained notoriety through dada artists, particularly Max Ernst, whose collages emerged early in the twentieth century in counterpoise to yet another intermedia form, the sentimental serial novel commercialized in nineteenth-century magazines. Ernst enjoyed, as Barthelme did, frequenting secondhand bookstores where he found a wealth of material for his collages in the newspapers and novels of the previous century. By decomposing and then reconstructing the melodramatic models, Ernst created his *romans-collages* in part to undercut the exaggerated emotional element of sentimental fiction and to "restore the dramatically poetic illustrations to their original banality."[18] Following Ernst's example, Barthelme reveled in his own duplicity.

Aside from halting dialogue, the textual fragments of Barthelme's "Eugénie Grandet" originate in letters and illustrations from Balzac's novel. These letters are always missives of bad news. The first in the novel is written by Charles's father to announce his financial ruin and impending suicide and to give charge of Charles's future to M. Grandet. As Barthelme splices the story together, he includes only a ragged piece of the letter, including the following shred:

> Part of a letter:
> . . . And now he's ruined, a
> friends will desert him, and
> humiliation. Oh, I wish I ha
> straight to heaven, where his
> but this is madness. . . .   (*SS,* 238)

The lofty tone of the original still survives, but the intended tragedy falters in motive and consequence. The reader may recall, moreover, that the unfinished letter in Balzac's story suspensefully omits the end, not the side, of the text.

Barthelme similarly mocks Eugénie's discovery of a second fatal letter. In Balzac's story, the subplot of Eugénie's love for Charles is captured by one illustrator in a scene in which Eugénie enters Charles's room (Caption: "The door stood ajar; she thrust it open"[19]). Charles slumps in a chair before a desk strewn with sealed letters. The exposed pages of the unfinished letter to Annette, however, glare at Eugénie. Barthelme undercuts this melodramatic moment by combining it with

Eugénie's perusal of the last letter in Balzac's work, a "Dear Cousin" note from Charles announcing his plan to marry a fortune. Investing Charles's letter with a rogue's indifference to Eugénie's grand sacrifice, Barthelme chips away the euphemistic language that varnishes Charles's intentions: "A brilliant life awaits," Charles writes, if he weds a girl "who is hideously ugly but possessed of a notable, if decayed, position in the aristocracy" (*SS*, 243). Finally, instead of fixing Eugénie's despair at this calamity by means of a sentimentalized illustration, Barthelme nonchalantly shifts the moment's focus from the grieving heroine to the cad who penned the letter. By accompanying his note with an expressionless "photograph" of Charles in the Indies, Barthelme, like Max Ernst, belies the contrivance of illustrative art and restores it to its "original banality." Other illustrations—a pencil outline of Eugénie's hand, a woodcut print of Eugénie holding a ball—similarly present the heroine as a simple, if spoiled, child, incapable of experiencing the tragic development that Balzac or his illustrator created for her.

In "Eugénie Grandet," parody shares with collage a shameless disrepute as subversive art. "One could say," writes an unabashed admirer of Ernst's work, "that collage is like the perfect crime" (Spies, 18). It succeeds by "diddl[ing] the manifest,"[20] by borrowing materials from works already in one form of print or another. Parody compounds the crime. Perhaps for this reason—that he felt he was not tending seriously enough to business—Barthelme omitted slapstick parody and pictorials from first-run short story collections after 1974. Still, he clearly heeded his father's advice: "Get out there and steal, but improve what you steal" (quoted in Ziegler, 52). If he is doubly guilty of these indiscretions in the 1974 volume, then his readers are loyal accomplices, for the writer's confession in the preface waves like a banner of virtue: "Guilty pleasures are the best" (*GP*).

Village Myths: Daedalus in Disguise "A Shower of Gold"

Though "A Shower of Gold," one of the most popular pieces from Barthelme's first collection, predates these formal parodies, it is the Janus of Barthelme's early work. Nodding toward both the contemporary crazes that provoke parody and Homer's distant gods, it mocks absurdity even as it chants its own myth. Those crazes include frantic searches for identity, the tyranny of dollars and cents over "private" values,[21] and particularly, Barthelme said, the individual's struggle to escape the net of professional languages. The self typically shrinks under these diabolical forces. As one character concludes, "The natural misfortune of our mortal and feeble condition is so wretched that when we consider it closely, nothing can console us" (*SS*, 20). In his quest to affirm his existence, therefore, the doubting protagonist Peterson must first acknowledge absurdity as the human condition, since the bizarre events of his own life daily confirm this predicament. Then, despite the humility of his diminished circumstances, he must defy the aggressors who would annihilate his soul, and will himself a measure of nobility.

Repeatedly, the story parodies the manufacturers of the "Hostile Object" who "respond to the world by adding to it constructs which are hostile to life."[22] Among these hostile constructs is a crew of fictional terrorists: the President destroys art with a six-pound sledge; Peterson's barber Kitchen rockets around jaws with his razor; a cat-piano player wields a switchblade and revels in the music howled by abused kittens. The creators of "Who Am I?," a parodic hybrid of "The Price Is Right," "What's My Line?," and "To Tell the Truth," add to the list of terrorist constructs a menacing lie-detector board, which threatens its subjects with accusing lights and bells until contestants confess that they are "alienated, desperate, living in anguish, despair and bad faith" (*SS*, 15). The humor of the original shows is darkened by the aggressive, existential line of questioning that reduces the contestants to shriven selves. They suffer nausea; they "feel *de trop*" (*SS*, 15). The interviewer warns Peterson, "We don't play around" (*SS*, 15).

But Peterson does. Though poor and out of favor with the public, Peterson refuses to prostitute his work on a commodity market where art is pitted against Chris-Crafts or to submit to his intimidators. Taking his turn with the monitors, Peterson begins to play his own game of "Who Am I?," making up answers even before the emcee can ask questions and ignoring threats on the cue cards: "In this kind of world . . . absurd if you will, possibilities nevertheless proliferate and escalate all around us. . . . Don't be reconciled. Turn off your television sets. . . . Visit girls at dusk. . . . How can you be alienated without first having been connected?" (*SS*, 22). Peterson challenges a desperate public to will themselves a better life. Then he invents his now-famous Olympian parentage (his mother, "a royal virgin"; his father, "a shower of gold" [*SS*, 22–23]) and extols his blissful rearing. His method, how-

17

ever, is still the doubling strategy of parody. Peterson plays against the rules of "Who Am I?" by reversing the usual question-and-answer format, by "lying" about his identity, and by adding, rather than stripping away, one mask after another. Furthermore, by inventing multiple possibilities for his life as a character, he plays against the audience's expectations that his *self*, like that of many others, can be diminished to a fixed, predictable, perhaps worthless existence.

"Barthelme's essential theme," William Stott believes, "is the human cost of a society that values publicity more than privacy. He shows us, quite simply, the danger in what we Americans are doing to ourselves with our faith in other people's values, our collectivist pleasures, our encounter groups and gropings, our lust for self-exposure" (382). But Peterson, Wayne Stengel adds, asserts the artist's alternative (54). He conceives a glorious birth in the image of Perseus—an identity created not from a decadent present, but from the residual memory of mankind's heroic, primordial past. Thus, he founds the pantheon of Barthelme's myth-makers.

"Bluebeard"

From Peterson, Barthelme's mythological beings and often their earthly counterparts inherit the elan of self-preservation. Though they are usually throwbacks to classical legends, their "scrabble for existence"—and that of the rest of us—is in the "here and now" (*SS*, 417), a present betrayed by its detritus, *blague*, and failed relationships. Like the wily Odysseus, Barthelme's displaced beings survive in contemporary landscapes by using cunning and sneak attack. Since ethics require public standards of morality, Barthelme ironically implies, his creatures may be excused, even applauded, for their sometimes unscrupulous behavior. More than one character, bloody hatchet or incriminating key in hand, winningly pleads, "Not my fault!" Witness Barthelme's tale of Bluebeard.

Barthelme explained that, in double-minded fashion, he recapitulated this grim children's story "from the perspective of one of the wives and potential victims," who is fully aware of both Bluebeard's "history" and her own precarious existence in the tale. As well educated in letters and manners as a Jane Austen heroine, she confesses a childlike infatuation for her notorious lover. After wooing her father's favor with rare gifts of art, he wins her heart with hypnotizing architectural sentiments and a black negligee. Not the garish shock of a beard, but an ebony nose, studding his 45-year-old visage like a hunk of silver-veined lava, belies his genteel manner, his aesthetic sensitivity. Still, during their first year of marriage, she defers to his every whim and shows no interest in using her silver key to open the one chamber prohibited her entrance. She seems obedient, loyal, afraid to tempt fate either by appearing malcontent or by crossing the forbidden portal into the room where the bloody baggage of six previous marriages might be stashed. By flatly ignoring his temptations, she keeps her health but also aggravates her scheming spouse. Maddened by her indifference, Bluebeard pauses thoughtfully; then he calls her "a peculiar woman" (*F*, 94).

The entire story pivots on this seemingly inconsequential description. Had she no knowledge of Bluebeard's legendary violence, yet still no wish to unlock the door, her lack of curiosity might have been "peculiar." Her guileless prototype in the original myth, for instance, could not resist the chamber's secrets. But in light of the "facts" that Barthelme's heroine possesses, obedience and suppressed curiosity are really quite reasonable, quite ordinary. So why does Bluebeard call her peculiar? More importantly, why do his wife's previously measured phrases suddenly dissipate into a feverish monologue, a complaint that she has had "no time to protest or plead [her] ordinariness" (*F*, 94)? Peering past the mask of girlish naïveté just before he spoke, Bluebeard must have glimpsed an extraordinarily complex woman, a woman capable of matching her husband's treachery. Until this moment, in fact, *she* has controlled the marriage, since her husband's behavior, consistent with the original myth, has been so predictable. Her feigned innocence has never provoked him to develop new strategies. Bluebeard, however, is suddenly wiser. After his cryptic gibe sires a "worm of doubt" (*F*, 94), she loses control and reveals her own contrivances in rapid succession.

Midway through the story, she mentions that concealment is Bluebeard's nature (the horrors behind the door, of course, but also, perhaps, his motive for giving her the silver key). Yet if the reader backtracks, he discovers that *her* dual nature has been evident all along. The reader's memory of the endangered damsel in the original myth initially enlisted his sympathies, but now, as Barthelme explained, her "wheeling and dealing" exposes her as "much more deceitful than her husband, in addition to turning the screw." Early in the story, she con-

19

fesses longing for a new motorcar but insists that she is too artless to devise a ruse to distract her husband's suspicions. Yet she immediately outlines a clever scheme: charm him with her seemingly inept driving (razing the roses) and thus disguise her lust for "great speed and dash" (*F*, 93). Later, she nonchalantly confides that she conceals 3, then 11 duplicate silver keys (a nervous wife might order one duplicate, but an expert dissembler calculates for risks and bad luck). Merely pretending obedience, she also delights in subtle annoyances and slams Blue-beard's croquet ball into the bushes. Most incriminating, though, is her cover-up of carnal intrigues: first, a liaison with a notorious Mexican revolutionary, "a well-known celibate with a special devotion to St. Erasmus of Delft, the castrate" (*F*, 95), she tells Bluebeard; second, a fiery affair with the castle chaplain, consummated in "midnight Sab-bats organized by the notorious Bishop of Troyes" (*F*, 96). Her proto-type in the original myth, in contrast, had prayed to delay execution. Mounting expressions of duplicity ("my shame and my delight," "un-holy yet cherished symbol" [*F*, 96]) complement further subterfuge—hiding a cache of love letters in the sanctuary altar, encoding secret messages to the Finance Minister, and stashing the codebook in her bicycle handlebars. Peculiar, indeed.

Despite these calculated betrayals, Bluebeard's wife charms the reader with her mischievous deeds, seemingly minor perversions in comparison to her husband's alleged atrocities. But as Barthelme re-veals her machinations, he simultaneously diminishes Bluebeard to a merry prankster. After she purposely "loses" her silver key, she ob-serves Bluebeard "trolling in the grass with a horseshoe magnet" (*F*, 94). Then, with boyish chagrin, he tells her that even a blackguard occasionally needs the "correction of connubial give-and-take" (*F*, 97). Finally, when she plunges into the fatal chamber, she discovers not the "rotting flesh" of her six predecessors' "beautifully dressed carcasses" (*F*, 94), but *seven* zebras, "gleaming in decay and wearing Coco Chanel gowns"—Bluebeard's "jolly" (*F*, 97) but long-delayed joke. She con-trarily faints "with rage and disappointment" (*F*, 97).

Unlike the original myth, Barthelme's story does not end with the villain's death and the damsel's happy-ever-after remarriage. As "Cri-tique de la Vie Quotidienne," the Edward and Pia stories, "Affection," and "Jaws" illustrate, marital bliss is itself a myth; "rage and disap-pointment," the too true reality. Perhaps Bluebeard and his wife are just an ordinary couple.

"Captain Blood"

According to Barthelme, "Captain Blood," "The Joker's Greatest Triumph," and "Engineer-Private Paul Klee" (a "little imaginary snapshot" of an art hero) spring chiefly from the "popular mythology" of American newspapers, television, and film rather than from Greco-Roman models or ancient folklore. "Sindbad," "The Phantom of the Opera's Friend," and even "Robert Kennedy Saved from Drowning" also fit this scheme. Honoring their classical ancestors, these stories' courageous if vulnerable heroes struggle, by duty, cape, or sword, to defend humanity's threadbare virtues—the only occupation they know. Their legendary stature never frees them from a moral obligation to inspire their ordinary kin.

A bit of homage to Sabatini and Errol Flynn's film role (O'Hara, 187–88), Barthelme's Captain Blood is a swashbuckling Renaissance man of a pirate, a Robin Hood salt, ethically bound to the glories of an old order. The order's rules are romantically enacted. Blood targets his prey and calculates the assault sequence; his men, a "grinning, leering, disorderly, rapacious crew," respectfully obey with "the strictest buccaneer discipline" (*F*, 199) because Blood posts a scale of booty bonuses including special compensation for the wounded. Blood's rigid code of honor similarly protects his female victims. When he thoughtlessly considers tossing women in the path of an enemy ship, he denounces himself as a vile idiot. Despite his rogue's lot, Blood also believes that he works under God's auspices to save the unwary: many poor souls "would have been stuck through the gizzard with a rapier, or smashed in the brain with a boarding pike, had it not been for Blood's swift, cheerful intervention" (*F*, 198). A buccaneer, often "pressganged" or "confined to the stinking dungeons of the Inquisition" for a trivial indiscretion, can sympathize with victims of such "monstrously unjust" (*F*, 200) but commonplace human evils.

Despite a "facade of steely imperturbability" (*F*, 197), only his romantic loyalty to timeworn values saves Captain Blood from a mythic midlife crisis. Though no Willy Loman, he frets over dwindling business and his crew's financial dependence on him. He needs new marketing strategies. Scanning the lonely seas, he pulls from his velvet coat pocket three mothballs and a 10-month-old memo: "*Dolphin*, Captain Darbraunce, 120 tons, cargo silver, paprika, bananas, sailing Mar. 10 Havana. *Be there!*" (*F*, 198). Even worse than slim prospects is frustration because his occasional prey seldom understands the buccaneer rules, or any rules at all. When "on land, Blood is confused and troubled by the life of cities," where strangers may assault him "for no reason" (*F*, 200). Merely steadying oneself among their teeming numbers, Blood shudders, is a "blistering occupation" (*F*, 200).

In the disorienting crush of city life, Blood, like the writers Barthelme describes in "Not-Knowing," suffers a "loss of reference" (*N*, 43). At sea, however, as in the focused structures of fiction, his small world harbors beautiful mysteries. His pleasures are simple: marmalade, perukes, enchanting names of captured ships, a cherished image of richly gowned women floating like iridescent lotuses in moonlit rainbows. Blood's treasures are Barthelme's tenderly chosen words, capable within wide margins of transforming the mundane world. Alone on the vast sea, though, Blood muses that shipboard exile, however romantic, is typically a narrow life: "One can be gallant all day long, and still end up with a spider monkey for a wife" (*F*, 202). The isolated Captain Blood risks preserving his riches in mothballs.

Yet sometimes Blood's world enlarges for a brief embrace with the chaotic hinterlands, just as Barthelme's fiction shares its mysteries with readers. Captain Blood is encouraged, for instance, when, during a routine raid, he discovers an "historical" heir to his legacy in the plucky American hero John Paul Jones. Whether Jones is a crusading patriot or a foolhardy "ninny" (*F*, 201), Blood admires the youthful captain's raw morals, his reckless determination to fight for his new country's honor. Jones is a man in his own image. In Jones, however, Barthelme issues another warning, this one reminiscent of "Report." Even after Blood promises Jones safe passage, the scrappy officer still insists on fighting; that is, Barthelme ironically implies, like an exemplary American, he invites a bloody assault "for no reason." The wiser Captain Blood corrects Jones's warmongering impulse before withdrawing once more into piracy's narrow cosmos.

Like the encounters between Jones and Blood, reader and author, the real and mythic worlds converge in the metaphorical rhythms that close Barthelme's story. Forming a ring that repeatedly widens and narrows, Captain Blood joins hands with his men and dances the "grave and haunting Catalonian *sardana*" (*F*, 202). Within the ocean's wide margins, all sway briefly as one "to the music of a single silver trumpet" (*F*, 202). If, as Barthelme lamented, the only common "world of reference" left to writers is a universe "in which the Love Boat [sails] on seas of passion like a Flying Dutchman of passion and the dedicated men in white of *General Hospital* pursue, with evenhanded diligence, triple bypasses, and the nursing staff" (*N*, 43), Captain Blood's poetic treasures momentarily restore some of the losses of discourse.

"Sindbad"

The close kinship of life's poor assaulted victims and Barthelme's self-perpetuating heroes is the explicit framework of "Sindbad." The story's narrator, a college instructor who has "never taught in the daytime before" (*F*, 28),[23] reels with confusion amid the campus's "enlightened" populace. As jaded and disarming as Peterson's intimidators, the narrator's students, like bored gossips at a cocktail party, scorn his appearance and then callously insist that he leave. At the Art and Architecture Departments' Ball, he is similarly rebuffed by an unidentifiable woman, who wears briefs emblazoned with a designer's name and calls herself Lady Macbeth. At night, the cleaning women and petty thieves become department czars, waging underworld business above the parking lot's "infernos of yellow light" (*F*, 32). Shellshocked, the instructor dons sunglasses to dim the world's harsh glare. Thus, he allies himself with other hiding men, Barthelme's other phantoms of the dark.

Initially, vignettes of Sindbad's bold adventures, alternating with the insecure narrator's feeble experiences, dramatize the distance between real and mythic worlds. As the story opens, "Sindbad, drowned animal, clutches at the sand of still another island shore" (*F*, 28). His sunburned skin attests to his glories in daylight. Unlike his stymied counterpart, Sindbad relishes a battle of wits with the inevitable "terrifying ogre" and expects to reap jewels "big as baseballs, which litter the ogre's domains, wonderfully" (*F*, 28). Furthermore, whereas the students demean anyone lacking a Camaro, fashion labels, and tweeds, Sindbad stocks his pearly emporium with "real goods . . . . the simple finest of everything" to make "lost, uncertain" (*F*, 30) people happy. Finally, undeterred by the cruel world's abuses, Sindbad relies on the promises and alternatives of his imagination: "But there is always a sturdy (wooden trough, floating beam, stray piece of wreckage from the doomed vessel) to cling to, and an island (garnished with rubies and diamonds, large quantities of priceless pearls, bales of the choicest ambergris) to pillage" (*F*, 33).

Until its conclusion, the story suggests little kinship between these characters. Attending the Beaux-Arts Ball, the narrator carries an En-

glish horn, his costume as one of "Robin Hood's merry men" (*F,* 30).
But this pretense to heroic gusto, hidden by night, is just foolish. At
the story's end, though, a circling dance once again fuses the ordinary
and mythic worlds. As Sindbad waltzes to new charms, the narrator
finally discovers his own life rhythm and begins teaching with the "heroic impertinence" (*F,* 33) of his mythic double. Sindbad, too, was
once poor, but he refused to relinquish his soul. This valuable moral
the now-invigorated narrator hopes to teach his disillusioned students.
Sunglasses removed, he holds the students with his "fiercest glare" (*F,*
34). Though they protest that there is "nothing out there" (*F,* 34), he
debunks their dark myth and enlightens them with possibility: "Be
like Sindbad! Venture forth! Embosom the waves, let your shoes be
sucked from your feet and your very trousers enticed by the frothing
deep. The ambiguous sea awaits . . . marry it!" (*F,* 34).

If Barthelme were ever guilty of stockpiling the world's trash in his
fiction, his lists of enchantments in "Captain Blood" and "Sindbad"
are apology enough. With literary gifts of "waltzes, sword canes, and
sea wrack dazzling to the eyes" (*F,* 34), Sindbad's double leads his
"lost, uncertain" students to the world's pearly emporium. Thus af-
firming his own valuable existence, he plunges with them "into the
Romantics" (*F,* 34) and life's "ambiguous sea."

Courting the Light

Set on more substantial terrain, numerous Barthelme stories focus his
criticism on collectivists who, refusing to be "cheered by the wine of
possibility and the growing popularity of light" cannot or will not make
"the leap" (*SS,* 379) into life's ambiguous but promising sea. In fact,
the darkness-into-light motif so explicit in "Sindbad" frequently reflects characters' denial or acceptance of the world. "The world in the
evening," pines one character, "seems fraught with the absence
of promise" (*SS,* 183). Equally shortsighted, the "Lightning" editor
cuts Connors's "lightning-as-grace" piece because "the *Folks* reader
[doesn't] like 'funny stuff'" (*F,* 180). On the other hand, forms of illumination, especially gold, glorify human riches: friendship, "the
most golden of the affections" (*SS,* 366); human love, "grisly and
golden as ever" (*SS,* 284); the dreamed-for father, "a shower of gold"
(*SS,* 23).[24] Artists often bear these torches. In "Opening," the play-
wright affectionately gives his actors "gold-wrapped chocolates" (*F,*
26), and when the world celebrates his artistic gifts, the notices sing,

"LIGHTS UP THE SKY . . . AND STIMULATES MEN'S MINDS" (*F,* 26).

As artistic illumination, music particularly heralds an awakening to, if not total acceptance of, life's possibilities. This music is not, of course, the comically redundant lyrics of "How I Write My Songs" (though the "Rudelle" record "became gold in 1976" [*SS,* 420]), but another form of grace. The reporter Connors, for instance, philosophizes, via an allusion to Nietzsche, that music redeems the world from failure and that lightning is God's music. Perhaps, therefore, he has a "song to sing" for the "burned beautiful creature" (*F,* 177) he adores. To Barthelme, however, the story "The New Music" was a "very depressing piece" (quoted in Ziegler, 58), for the two characters deny "new life," "new hope" (*SS,* 339). Barthelme fretted, "I worry about these two men. . . . They are separated from all notions of, or all belief in, progress in the world" (quoted in Ziegler, 57–58). Having learned by rote what "Momma didn't 'low" (*SS,* 342), they fear provoking the haunt of her "dark side" (*SS,* 347). Hence, they defer listening to the new music until "tomorrow and tomorrow and tomorrow" (*SS,* 349).

In "The Leap," when one character asserts, "Purity of heart is to will one thing" (*SS,* 384), his more visionary companion corrects him: "No. . . . Purity of heart is, rather, to will several things, and not know which is the better, truer thing, and to worry about this, forever" (*SS,* 384). Here speaks the strongest voice of Barthelme's myths but one that too often is silenced by the collectivists' drone. In the following three sketches, the protagonists—one spiritual mentor, two artists—are characters most capable of enlightening the masses but also most vulnerable to banishment or annihilation.

"The Temptation of St. Anthony"

"The Temptation of St. Anthony" plays against deflated religious mythology. Like the *Folks* readers, the story's collectivists deny "ineffable" (*F,* 149) experiences, which cannot be reduced to simple, concrete terms. Compelled "to get all opinions squared away with all other opinions, or at least in recognizable congruence with the main opinion," they refuse "to imagine the marvelous" (*F,* 151). Scrutinizing St. Anthony's apartment, for instance, they find no evidence of peculiar godlike habits, just the standard beige carpet, brown bedspread, and hint of fried foods. In the world's eye St. Anthony's act of inviting a mugger to take his Bulova, moreover, quickly marks him as much a simpleton as a saint. Still, in the "world of mundanity . . . he *shone*" (*F*, 156). Resentful citizens, therefore, try to discredit his extraordinary reputation with earthly temptations. Even after he has abandoned city comforts, a few errant wise men visit his desert hovel to bear him useless consumer gifts, while those hoping to nail him to the postlapsarian family tree accuse him of sexual misconduct.

Ironically, though the narrator fancies himself an emissary between the mundane and the marvelous, he also tries "to normalize" (*F*, 151) St. Anthony. In contrast to the resentful masses, however, he excuses or rationalizes the latter's inconsistencies, never fully understanding why St. Anthony's "major temptation" is "ordinary life" (*F*, 152). At first, the saint's alleged promiscuity makes the narrator squirm. Rumor and innuendo cheapen St. Anthony's advances to a shapely philosophy student. But then "sexual things" (*F*, 154) have always baffled the narrator. Eventually, he defends St. Anthony's behavior as providence, squaring it with charismatic opinion: "Sexuality is as important as saintliness, and maybe as beautiful, in the sight of God, or else why was it part of the Divine plan?" (*F*, 155). He similarly interprets St. Anthony's curiosity concerning a radio as nostalgia for the sacred music of the spheres. Though the narrator wants to believe in the extraordinary, he neither imagines for himself the inherent appeal of "ordinary life," nor understands the alternatives illumined by St. Anthony's final word: "Or" (*F*, 153). St. Anthony may be forced into desert isolation, but the city's collective citizens are the true hiding men.

"The Phantom of the Opera's Friend"

"The Phantom of the Opera's Friend" is another transformation of popular myth with parodic overtones. First, aside from the obvious debt to Gaston Leroux's story, the hiding artist and his urban confidant bear striking resemblance to Poe characters: like Roderick Usher, who is also tended by a well-intentioned but naive friend, the Phantom dwells in dark, gothic chambers; indulges his aesthetic interests; has an insufferable sensitivity to light; and exhibits radical mood swings with a propensity for melancholy. Second, through a curious role reversal for Barthelme's characters, Phantom and friend pay homage to Dante. Bitter passions—anger, jealousy, revenge—have exiled the scarred specter to Stygian night "five levels below the Opera, across the dark lake" (*SS*, 138). With theft and extortion to his discredit, he counts other sins as well. However, bearing friendship's golden torch, his Virgilian guide counsels the Phantom in earthly wisdom and beseeches him to ascend into the light. A "new life," "many satisfactions," and "possibility" require only "the will to break out of old patterns" (*SS*, 140). The Phantom must share with the world his glorious music, a haunting double of Purgatory's harmonies. Even its thin echo from the Opera's gloomy recesses thrills the narrator. But like Dante's doomed souls, the Phantom lacks will.

Ironically, the Phantom is as self-contradictory as any of the ambiguities he resists. He cannot decide "whether to risk life aboveground or to remain forever in hiding" (*SS*, 139). During his cautious nocturnal ventures into the city, only fragments of the streetlamps' glow or lightning briefly illumine him. His friend's exhortations, moreover, are just a "flicker" (*SS*, 140) in his thoughts. Yet the narrator's promises of possibility are also misleading. Having arranged for a plastic surgeon "to normalize" the Phantom, the friend prepares a bright room with velvet curtains to ease the recluse's adaptation to light. But he has been duped by science's "album of magical transformations" (*SS*, 142).

The surgeon's gleaming scalpel would deliver the Phantom from darkness only to diminish him to beauty's common run. A "qualified alienist" (*SS*, 142) would similarly shrink his psyche. The psychiatrist resembles not only the analyst in "The Sandman," but also Edward, the handwriting analyst in "Margins." Edward insists that he is "communicating . . . across a vast gulf of ignorance and darkness" when he generalizes that the wide margins on his companion Carl's sign betoken "a person of extremely delicate sensibilities with love of color and form, one who holds aloof from the multitude and lives in his own dream world of beauty and good taste" (*SS*, 9). But as Barthelme implies in such stories, society's analysts paradoxically steal, rather than deliver, their subjects' dreams. The alienation of Carl, the Phantom, and other beings is the error not of artistic eccentricity, but of the collectivists' unilateral vision.

"Engineer-Private Paul Klee Misplaces an Aircraft Between Milbertshofen and Cambrai, March 1916"

Through another role reversal, the recluses in "Engineer-Private Paul Klee" are the collective Secret Police, a melancholy lot who "exist in the shadows" of their "dismal service" (*F*, 84). Fearful of life's contradictions and uncertainties, they long for godlike absolutes: "omniscience . . . omnipresence . . . omnipotence" (*F*, 81). Yet they are ordinary beings. Despite their claims to ubiquity, their "trained policemen's eyes" (*F*, 82) see only Paul Klee. They are as befuddled as he is when one of the three canvas-covered aircraft Paul Klee has been transporting mysteriously disappears in broad daylight. While indecision immobilizes his stalkers, however, Paul Klee studies the enigma with his "trained painter's eye" (*F*, 81–82) and considers his possibilities. Paradoxically, reason solves the absurdity: with "painter's skill," which is "not so different from a forger's" (I will resist making any comparison to Hephaestus), he decides to "diddle the manifest" (*F*, 83). Hence, he conceals the canvas and ropes that would signify the third aircraft's loss. He then rewards himself with chocolate.

The Secret Police's approval of Paul Klee's ruse suggests kinship between the artist and his observers. Yet just as they can only wish for godlike authority, they can only pretend camaraderie with the mythic hero. Unlike Captain Blood and Sindbad, their trinity steps a fixed "three-sided waltz" (*F*, 81); confined to darkness by their own fear and ignorance, they "are not embraceable" (*F*, 84). But Paul Klee delights in the small pleasures of his sunlit, ambiguous world. Uncertainty about the translation of some "slight and lovely" (*F*, 81) Chinese stories does not undermine his reading enjoyment. Ultimately, the frustration of the missing aircraft is also negligible. Enchanted by the beauty manifested in its absence, he sketches the suggestive remains—"the canvas forming hills and valleys, seductive folds, the ropes the very essence of looseness, lapsing" (*F*, 82). The sketch, in turn, recalls pleasurable hotel liaisons with Lily.

Like St. Anthony's hostile spies and the Secret Police, Barthelme's characters too frequently deny or misconstrue their affiliation with saints, angels, gods, and even artists. Yet as the narrator of "On Angels" explains, "It is a curiosity of writing about angels [or saints or gods] that, very often, one turns out to be writing about men. The themes are twinned" (*SS*, 136). Without an absolute creator to order the unknown, for instance, angels, "unaccustomed to terror, unskilled in aloneness" (*SS*, 135), despair as do some mortals. Neither the angels' lustrous garments nor the Secret Police's boasts about superior intelligence match Paul Klee's humble insights. Rather than defeat himself with impossible, large-scale attempts to perfect or control his world (alone, he cannot stop war), Paul Klee is content with small gifts of happiness: mankind's insanity is temporary, but "drawings and chocolate go on forever" (*F*, 84).

In "Not-Knowing," Barthelme promoted art's "meliorative" responsibility: "Art thinks ever of the world, cannot not think of the world,
could not turn its back on the world even if it wished to" (50). Reiter-
ating this point in our 1988 interview, he explained that, like Sindbad's
double and Paul Klee, a writer may wage a constructive quarrel with
the world, even if the reward is only a small coup—a "butterfly effect,
something very small but which nevertheless has over time some con-
sequences." Though often comic meditations, Barthelme's parodies
and myths exploit double vision's possibilities. With diddle and flutter,
they not only change perception, but dare to change the world.

Possibility in a "World Made New"

In "After Joyce" (1964) Barthelme confidently asserted that "the literary object is itself 'world' and the theoretical advantage" of pondering a rock on this new terrain "is that in asking it questions you are asking questions of the world directly" (13). But not everyone bought art's excuse for strangeness, and almost 20 years later Barthelme himself admitted that when he wrote the proposition, he was somewhat "beguiled by the rhetoric of the time" (*N*, 49). Editing first the University of Houston *Forum* and then *Location* had steeped him in the persuasive dreams of contemporary artists and philosophers, whose words illumined these journals' pages. But even if his idealistic revelry in "the new" ultimately garnered the metafictional tag that so annoyed him, the indebtedness of Barthelme's fiction to such sources can hardly be exaggerated. Whenever he listed literary influences—Joyce, Beckett, Hemingway, Kafka, Sabatini, Perelman—he also nodded homage to masters in other genres.

Barthelme's work is everywhere pressed with the art world's touch. During his youth, harmonies of classical music tempered the family home's Mies architecture, and Barthelme frequented black nightclubs, where he applauded the jazz kings' creative variations on trite tunes (O'Hara, 185). As lyric performances in "The Jazz King" demonstrate, music's seemingly inexhaustible orchestrations prompted him to experiment with the pitch, tone, chords, rhythms, and antiphonal choirs of mixed speech levels. Similarly, years of reviewing films for the *Houston Post* and the University of Houston *Cougar* yielded his cinematic manipulation of narrative viewpoint. But his move to New York City in 1962 initiated his most significant tutelage. According to Barthelme, over scandalous lunches and on afternoon jaunts to galleries, museums, and studios, Tom Hess and Harold Rosenberg schooled him in both abstract expressionism and the poetics of Ashbery, Koch, and Schuyler. After his mentors' deaths in 1978, Barthelme continued these pilgrimages, particularly to SoHo and East Village galleries. He also wrote catalog introductions for Mary Boone and Rauschenberg shows. To Rauschenberg's collages and found objects, he attributes in part the complex structures of his most perplexing stories. By saddling a goat with a tire, Rauschenberg invested otherwise ordinary objects with magic: no one can resolve the contradictions of that odd merger (*N*, 45–46). Barthelme hoped to conjure words with equal sorcery.

Often citing his debt to visual artists, he likened his stories to spare but provocative paintings. "I've been told by a neurologist," he mused, "that writing comes from the left brain in right-handed people and painting from the right brain, so I'm glad our brains may be getting together."[25] Still, he envied the "metaphysical advantage" of painters—their materials' "physicality" and their freedom from language's signifying demands. People might cheer de Kooning for smearing charcoal into paint with his gifted thumb, he quipped, but a writer who smudges language elicits nothing but boos (O'Hara, 199). Yet in a symposium with Grace Paley, Walker Percy, and William Gass, he did concede that writers have one "immense" edge: "Painting is normally an object on a wall, and you go up to it and look at it and you don't look at it for very long; whereas we, if we are successful, get somebody and hold on to him for a certain length of time" (*SF*, 25). Ironically, though they are not as easily manipulated as paint on canvas, Barthelme's words snag their prey, intrigue him with their "physicality." When they are promiscuously "allowed to go to bed together" (*N*, 48), Barthelme wrote, words rivet the voyeur—even solicit him in their play.

The Collage Text: Postmodern Architecture "To London and Rome"

Barthelme's initial efforts to redesign plot's architecture with spatial patterns are sometimes labored and self-conscious. An early collage experiment, "To London and Rome" (*CB*, 159–69) rends plot into two simultaneous narratives. Claiming almost three-fourths of each page's textual space, the story proper catalogs Peter and Alison's obsessive purchasing and jokes toward a conclusion as rapidly as Peter can write checks. Conversely, in the pages' narrow left-hand columns idle all the pauses, intervals, and silences that might delay the contrived plot. Frustrating the reader's habitual left-to-right march across the page, the story generates horizontal, vertical, and diagonal cross-references.

Shortly after Alison and Peter buy a concert grand piano in the story proper, for instance, they discuss calling a piano instructor, learn they are overdrawn at the bank, and then leave for breakfast. Peter also ignores Alison's come-hither look. In the left-hand column, however, lurk a silence thick with sex, the couple's interlude in bed, and phone calls ordering a piano teacher and a piano tuner. If the reader disregards the narrative on the left to follow the predominant story, he misses not only the sex scene, but also the phone calls (Alison and Peter miss out as well). Consequently, when two mysterious strangers later appear unannounced in the living room on the right, the reader must backtrack, take a diagonal leap to the left-hand margin, and mentally collate his findings in order to verify the intruders' identities.

With such heavy-handed, comic disruptions, Barthelme offers several possibilities for superimposing the alternative stories, but the process suffers limits, since "To London and Rome" still relies on plot to mesh its narrative parts. A tire variously yokes, belts, or shackles a goat. We note the anomaly and pass on. Certainly, more provocative displacements occur when Barthelme minimizes linear sequence to diddle verb tense, tone, speech patterns, and point of view. As he refines these prismatic designs, he borrows other artists' advantages, too.

"The Wound"

Adapting cinematic technique to his fiction, Barthelme creates subtle exchanges among his texts' linguistic fragments by shrinking, blurring, or enlarging their properties. Barthelme's audience has to learn to read this sort of composition in the same way that audiences had to learn to assimilate the fragments of a film, "to follow a narrative line through a sequence of truncated images—torsos cut off at the waists, disembodied hands and heads, fragments of rooms and landscapes."[26] "The Wound" dramatizes this process. The story assembles a parodic cross section of disaffected Hemingway personnel: a torero with a gored foot and a fetish for his mother's hair; a mistress who habitually sheds her blouse; the torero's Lysol-packing mother; an aficionado of bulls and breasts; the Bishop of Valencia; the Queen of the Gypsies; and a host of parasitic "*imbéciles, idiotas,* and *bobos*" (*F,* 115). Barthelme then confines his unlikely characters to a studio set. Though they may enter and exit, the narrative camera never moves from its original position. On stage, moreover, the mistress and the mother imitate their creator by taking home movies of the story's verbal images.

Like the viewer of a film, the reader sees only "partialized space with parts of the object severed from the whole by the frame of the camera" (Spiegel, 37). In one paragraph's successive shots, for instance, the reader views the arrival of a telegram defaming the torero, the mistress removing her shirt, the mother's scowl at the imbéciles, and the torero's head flopping into a bobo's hands. Without narrative guidance, the reader might hastily dismiss these shots as gratuitous gestures—the mistress's indiscretion, say, as the compulsive behavior of an amoral exhibitionist or the torero's collapse as professional despair, a misfortune that has estranged his mistress. She now seeks attention from the doltish visitors. The mother does not approve. But as further shots isolate, enlarge, and accumulate each character's eccentricities, the story bristles with contradictions. In another fragment, for example, the mistress, apparently ashamed for the Bishop to see her bare breasts, self-consciously dons her blouse. What tales, what moral, psychological, or philosophical truths can the reader imagine to explore the mistress's discrepancies or the Bishop's nightmares or the disgruntled bobos' jealousy of upper-crust privileges? Where and how do these lives overlap? Now Barthelme offers far more than the bearded goats and slick tires of a spliced plot.

Objects within his viewfinder are similarly disconcerting. Frequently zooming in on a hunk of roast beef, the torero's blades, and the bloody stigma, the camera seemingly endows props with symbolic value. The characters themselves exaggerate these distortions. The mother, playing with her zoom lens, films the torero's gaping wound, which the reader has already viewed when the foot's goring was televised "first at normal speed, then in exquisite slow motion" (*F*, 116). In addition, the bobos sublimate their desire for the mistress's breasts by salivating over the roast beef. Finally, the Queen of the Gypsies galvanizes the icons. After thrusting her knife into the roast beef, she gnaws on torn meat, while she savors the torero's wound. She then claims both wound and attached torero as her own. The collage thus coheres through the interplay of imagined tales and suggestive motifs.

"Our Work and Why We Do It"

In "Our Work and Why We Do It," a studio set again summons Barthelme's characters, but this time romantic fetishes secure their affinity. In a printing office, dedicated typographers fret over the ink color, typeface, and dot structure of their various creations (matchbook covers, the currency of Colombia, Alice Cooper T-shirts, criminals' fingerprints), while the owners, William and Rowena, scandalize their colleagues by fiddling around in a nearby bed. Despite the context's incongruity, at least one motif weds the collective fragments: the owners' promiscuity recapitulates the narrator's love for his work. The narrator admits that he cannot keep his hands off the exquisite typefaces, paraded down the page like exotic beauties for the reader to admire:

Annonce Grotesque

Compacta

Cooper Black

Helvetica Light

(*SS*, 320)

His job, he says, is "to kiss the paper with the form or plate" (*SS*, 319).

In this story, Barthelme's lens frames not only actions and speeches, but also thoughts. Defying the spatial limits of viewpoint, the first-person narrator films all textual flow, including his colleagues' musings; similarly, temporal disruptions shatter conventional flashback. In one scene, for instance, the narrator records the silent reminiscences of an aging senior printer. As the latter reflects on the toils and troubles of a printer's work in the old days, the fragmented text simulating his revery performs jump cuts. Disconnected phrases suggest glimpses of a Wells Fargo man, his .38, a safe's knobs and precious contents—not gold, however, but the recently printed Alice Cooper T-shirts. Then, swiftly juxtaposed with the printer's reminiscences race the narrator's truncated thoughts: a weeping woman in a brown Mercedes; past and current production problems; and, close by, pressman Percy handing a yellow ink can to William, one of the owners.

"William," this scene's last word, nudges immediately into the next fragment. It begins, "William was sitting naked in the bed wearing the black hat" (*SS*, 318), and the reader prepares to move through further visual/aural motifs of the "situation." William then periodically utters "Yesterday." Like the old printer's safe, the word "yesterday" secures precious memories, private thoughts. Eventually, though, it yields William's fantasy about saving hot dog vendors from the city police by galloping to their rescue with lariats, .30–30s, and his black hat. His spoken anecdote recalls two familiar images from the earlier scene: William wearing the black hat in bed and the printer's silent western revery. Once again, the text lassoes all yesterdays into an ongoing present, while disconnected fragments reflect the narrator's passion for the look and sound of words, a passion shared by Barthelme.

Repetitive hooks like those noted in both "The Wound" and "Our Work and Why We Do It" also hinge textual fragments in other comparatively more abstract stories. In "Cortés and Montezuma," for instance, each scene features a slightly different arrangement of the main personages in iconographic association with one or more repeated emblems: a green fly, a golden-wired whisk, a hurled stone. Then, as in "Our Work and Why We Do It," familiar phrases superimpose a scene's text on a related fragment, though not necessarily a text nearby. In "Cortés and Montezuma," this hooking pattern occurs each of the nine times personages stroll "down by the docks" (*SS*, 328). Fragments in these stories cohere through what Roland Barthes calls "a fugal continuity, in the course of which identifiable fragments ceaselessly reappear"[27] but in different combinations. Repetition's familiarity encourages readers to participate in the artistic process, but the "not-knowing" sustains its mystery. According to Barthelme, the magic of such a text, like Rauschenberg's infamous artwork, "is that it at once invites and resists interpretation. Its artistic worth is measurable by the degree to which it remains, after interpretation, vital—meaning that no interpretation or cardiopulmonary push-pull can exhaust or empty it" (*N*, 46).

"See the Moon?" and "On the Deck"

Discovering these hooks in Barthelme's texts is an ambitious but delightful enterprise. Still, Barthelme explained, minimalist tactics are risky. If a writer's words look funny on the page, the faint of heart abandon him. The "lunar hostility" (*SS*, 97) monitor in "See the Moon?" dealt Barthelme considerable trouble when he confessed, "Fragments are the only forms I trust" (*SS*, 98), since this debility seemed the author's handicap. The character's patchy autobiography, in fact, catalogs distorted elements of Barthelme's life: the ancestral ball player, a successful father, a post-truce stint in Korea, writing "poppycock" (*SS*, 98) for a university president, the envy of painters' advantages, a failed marriage, a mad affinity for light. Consequently, since the narrator can only wish that these historical bits, like the hodgepodge of mementos pinned to his wall, will "someday merge, blur—cohere is the word, maybe—into something meaningful" (*SS*, 98), more than one reader has questioned the author's vision. Yet perhaps such skeptics miss "the most essential thing" (*SS*, 106). Even the "knowledgeable knowers knowing" (*SS*, 107) deliver their evidence piecemeal.

As "See the Moon?" opens, the narrator mentions how viewing the night sky through a screen door graphs the cratered orb, spatially subdivides its mystery into tiny compartments of light. The grid allows him to zoom in on one or another surface, but if he squints, the fragments "merge, blur—cohere." Though he cannot explain this lunar enigma any more than he can resolve his own life's ambiguities, he has a *sense* of an ephemeral whole. Like all visionary beings, he, the artist, and we must attend to edges: his airplane's folded edges, the world's edges (Columbus's secret worry), and the story's edges—those places where Barthelme's words touch, blur, momentarily cohere. The narrator's wisdom particularly illuminates pieces like "On the Deck." This story is a frame tale, but, ironically, instead of developing a plot within a plot, it paints pictures within pictures, films scenes within scenes. The story invites mixing media and metaphors.

"On the Deck" pans across a little tugboat of humanity, yet when the story opens, the cameraman has apparently deserted the set. With only the celluloid strip before him, the reader must examine his findings alone, a still frame at a time. Moving so slowly, he can think about the pictures, note the edges. In the first frame lounges a washed out lion, a weary beast that will later roll its head like the MGM mascot. Literally subdivided by another of Barthelme's grids into 64 lion squares, his fragmented image dramatizes the story's design. A primary-color motif, refracted through a "PRISMATEX" (*F*, 15) label and fanned by a peacock elsewhere on deck, relates the visually charged pictures. Notably, splashes of red brighten the motorcyclists' bandanas, a partially covered Camry, a man's bloodied shirt, the captain's face, a mail lady's hair, another man's wicker chair. Similarly, yellow, muted in the lion's tawny coat and a bucket of liver, glints from the bikers' earrings and beckons from a young woman's "thin thin yellow dress" and her sister's "yellow shorts" (*F*, 15). Blue, however, tints more than just the bloodied shirt's stripes or the mail lady's uniform: it is the pall of the disconnected characters' loneliness.

Were the film speeded up, the frames would offer at least an illusion of coherence. Without overt interaction, however, the various odd figures seem just decorative props, surrealistically poised on a picture plane. The Jesus gang, "a sweetness expressed in the tilt of their bodies toward the little girl wearing shiny steel leg braces" (*F*, 14), lean near their inspiration, but they never touch her. Characters occasionally speak, but they elicit no responses. Where are humanity's bonds? The answer shimmers in the colors' touch. At the picture-story's center, where the thinly clad woman bends over the yellow PRISMATEX drum, a voice suddenly instructs us, "Concentrate on the hams" (*F*, 15). To this point, the clinical narration has droned like a prerecorded message, with no particular interest encouraged for one picture over another. Now, as the hams sway with the ship's tilt, the red-faced captain confides his need for "encouragement" and then "kisses the hem" (*F*, 15) of the young woman's gossamer dress. Similarly, as the woman's sister squats to cook hot dogs, a "bag of buns" near her foot, her boyfriend plays with the "bottom edge of her yellow shorts" (*F*, 15). A morning's pleasure, he intimates, depends on her mercy and her moods: "At some point you get into it pretty far, then it becomes frightening" (*F*, 15). But his voice, like the captain's, wafts into the silent sea air.

Though the narrative immediately resumes its deadpan catalog of the deck's figures, the men's thwarted yearning for these bright beings unmistakably informs the next frustrated confession: "I put two forty-pound sacks of cat food in the bed . . . but she still didn't get the message" (*F*, 16). Blocked messages, silent rejections, dead letters on deaf ears—all finally culminate in the mail lady's delivery to the captain, the bikers, Liverman, "the woman in the scandal-dress," and a "man sitting in a red wicker chair" (*F*, 16). "Everyone gets mail" (*F*, 16), yet some fear the empty envelope.

A winter of discontent next whitens the deck scene but as quickly thaws in spring's blazing sun. The reason for this yellow-red flood exclaims itself in the final picture, as suddenly requited passion releases the frozen frames from their present-tense suspension: "You came and fell upon me, I was sitting in the wicker chair. . . . You were light, I thought, and I thought how good it was of you to do this. We'd never touched before" (*F*, 16). As the reader now discovers, the story's primary relationship beams not only in its colors, but in the happy couple's tumble. For one light moment, the spatially poised figures "merge, blur—cohere . . . into something meaningful."

"A Woman Seated on a Plain Wooden Chair . . ."

According to William Gass, as the contemporary writer's words preempt other media on spatial planes, they "descend into flesh, into sound and shape" (*SF*, 24). Clearly, Barthelme covets the exotic word lists in "Our Work and Why We Do It" and "Cortés and Montezuma." Nowhere, however, is the "physicality" of his language more tangibly seductive than in this intriguing bridge piece from *Overnight to Many Distant Cities*. The collection includes several such "prose poems." "They called for more structure . . ." opens the volume with a hymn to the writer's "radiant" cities of words: "Babel, Chandigarh, Brasilia, Taliesin."[28] A builder who has worked on these projects lauds the architect's "ferocious integrity of . . . detailing" (*O*, 10). Below him, the new city glows in "the shape of the word FASTIGIUM," not the city's name, but a mystical structure chosen for the "elegance of the script" (*O*, 10). The city's intense aura even resurrects a small child, "dead behind the rosebushes" (*O*, 10). A similarly mystical piece, "A woman seated on a plain wooden chair . . ." creates breath and flesh in letters' illusory shapes.

Like the detached cameraman in "On the Deck," a fastidious narrator describes the composition's details, one frame or painted panel at a time. In this piece, however, each paragraph's view selects and rearranges the opening scene's visually charged images. Standing with the narrator in front of a picture plane, for instance, we first see a woman in white overalls, two German shepherds, Benvenuto Cellini, and "a row of naked women kneeling, sitting on their heels, their buttocks as perfect as eggs or O's—OO OO OO OO OO OO OO" (*O*, 67). Hereafter, buttocks loom sensuously wherever zeroes or capital *O*'s recur in the remaining textual fragments. The second paragraph subtly suggests this connection. Each of two women "wrapped as gifts" (*O*, 67) holds a white envelope; the envelopes, this image intimates, contain a pair of letters (*OO*'s?) for Tad. The next two paragraphs enhance the illusion. Two naked women, their hair rolled in "buns," their bodies splashed with blue paint, dramatize the medium's physicality: one nymph drags the other across white paper, while rows of spectators view the process. The image twins the layout on the page.

Provocative *O*'s now frequently soar before the reader's eyes, whether they are literally printed or not. The fifth paragraph begins, "Nowhere—the middle of it, its exact center" (*O*, 68). As Edgar Allan Poe explains in "The Philosophy of Composition," *O* is a sonorous vowel, whose lingering pronunciation extends its role. Hence, the center of *nowhere* is not really the *h*, but the protracted vowel. For doubters or hasty readers, Barthelme provides two additional hooks. At the center of *nowhere*, the text says, is "the word PHONE" (*O*, 68)—now what is in the middle?—and the telephone system's symbol, a blue ring around a bell. Both color and shapes recall the previous fragments. Appropriately, therefore, two naked women, breasts and thighs touching, stand inside this structure—a "booth" (*O*, 68, italics my own)—while Benvenuto Cellini, dressed in white overalls, lingers nearby.

The paragraphs that follow similarly exchange suggestive elements. In the "world of work" (*O*, 68), the text simulates buttocks not only when it reprints two pairs of *O*'s for the naked ladies perched on lofty stools, but also each time the word *Or* introduces an alternative job position, like bending over an architectural site in the "Camer*oo*ns" or teaching Naked Physics I and II in contiguous "class*roo*m[s]" (*O*, 68–69, italics my own). To this fragment's end, the sensuous figures have been alluring but aesthetically benign. In the story's last two passages, though, a pair of women bundled in parkas and blue caps inspects a row of certainly blue prey.

From hooks in a frigid meat locker dangle "naked satyrs, hairy-legged, split-footed, tailed and tufted" (*O*, 69), perhaps the voyeurs implied in the previous passages. This vulgar display now toys visually with the text through the locker's temperature reading—"a constant 18 degrees" (*O*, 69). The vertical alignment of *O*'s in the *8* imitates the satyrs' positions; visualizing the degree symbol next to the number (18°) also conjures their tufted tails. The story's initially austere tone is just as violently upended. With goading from a raucous female audience, the two women force their victims to "squirm and dance" by "tickling" them "under the tail, where they are most vulnerable" (*O*, 69–70). As the satyrs writhe in pain or pleasure, the story's last line completes the fiction's transformations. The opening paragraph's "buttocks as perfect as eggs or O's" now enlarge menacingly: "giant eggs, seated in red plush chairs, boil" (*O*, 70).

Despite its abstractions, this piece bares the sexes' obsessions and conspiracies as articulately as any mythical or realistic sketches of the connubial cocoon.

Interior Designs
"Views of My Father Weeping"

The critiques offered thus far chiefly explore Barthelme's artistic alternatives for plot. As "See the Moon?" and "Our Work and Why We Do It" indicate, unless narrative voice emits from a detached observer, a piece's central character can radiate instabilities equal to those of story lines. Barthelme constructs "Views of My Father Weeping," for instance, through a first-person narrator who recapitulates one story—an aristocrat's act of running over his father—from infinite perspectives (the story ends "Etc." [*SS*, 126]). Here, interspersing past-tense vignettes with multiple views of the deceased patriarch simulates collage's temporal and spatial ambiguity.

Two paradoxes account for this ambiguity. First, despite reports to the contrary, the father does not seem dead at all because his corporeal image pops up mischievously among the variant plots. The reader must therefore reconcile his omnipresence with the alleged casualty. Second, since no *one* report clarifies the calamity's "truth," the reader must likewise accept all narrative views simultaneously. Lars Bang, the infamous coachman accused of driving the deathwagon, delivers the incident's last and most notorious reconstruction. After denying any wrongdoing and implicating the father as a drunkard and malcontent, Lars assures the narrator that *his* version puts the bereaved son "in possession of all the facts" (*SS*, 126). Immediately, however, a sultry girl insists, "Bang is an absolute bloody liar" (*SS*, 126). A black dot and "Etc." then herald a shift to tales ad infinitum. Unable to discount any testimony or to align the contrary viewpoints in chronological order, the reader must shape a mental collage in which the multiple vignettes vie not only with each other, but also with the incongruous views of the father.

Hoping to resolve this maze of plots and disconcerting portraits, the reader looks to the narrator to distinguish the fiction's real entrance and exit from its false ones. Yet the protean narrator is equally fallible. Struggling to evade grief and guilt for his father's loss, the narrator effects his own displacements. First, he projects himself into the past as a detective, so that he may reconstruct the accident's events with scientific objectivity. Spinning off detached accounts, he performs his filial duty without sorrow or remorse. However, another displacement occurs against his will when he abruptly lurches into a present-tense fiction staged on an interior plane of feeling. Here, his performance is tentative. In a weak attempt to defuse his emotions, he rationalizes that the figure before him is someone else's father. But as his attention focuses on the man's weeping, the narrator's own despair threatens to surface: "It is someone's father. That much is clear. He is fatherly. The gray in the head. The puff in the face. The droop in the shoulders. The flab on the gut. Tears falling. Tears falling. Tears falling. Tears falling. More tears. . . . O lud lud! But why remain? Why watch it? Why tarry? Why not fly? Why subject myself?" (*SS*, 118). Distressed by this scene, the narrator flees the emotions that the father image evokes. His only escape is to displace himself in yet another fictitious role.

Donning his actor's plumed hat, he now poses as an outraged son seeking reprisal for his father's honor. The abrupt shift in roles rallies a corresponding shift in tone and style to the hyperbole of revenge tragedy: "Why! . . . there's my father! . . . sitting in the bed there! . . . and he's *weeping!* . . . as though his heart would burst! . . . Father, please! . . . look at me, Father . . . who has insulted you? . . . are you, then, compromised? . . . ruined? . . . a slander is going around? . . . an obloquy? . . . a traducement? . . . 'sdeath! . . . I won't permit it! . . . I won't abide it! . . . I'll . . . move every mountain . . . climb every river . . . etc." (*SS*, 121). As the last word suggests, this view, like all the fiction's perspectives, will be repeatedly displaced among the text's alternative structures.

For the most part, however, the multiple identities of "I"—objective reporter, relentless detective, filial avenger—minimally disrupt the fiction. The various personae are so familiar from conventional fiction that the reader spontaneously fleshes them out with what other narratives have taught him to expect of these roles. But when the father/son images occasionally merge, the task is not so simple. This permutation of the first-person narrator occurs each time the son fails to escape his feelings into a distant past. The father then haunts the narrator as a strange composite of youth and old age. He fits the general concept of "father"—graying hair, puffy face, pouchy stomach—but his behavior is infantile. Alternate views depict him writing on the wall with his crayons, jamming his thumb into pink cupcakes, or clumsily thrusting his adult hand into a doll's house and knocking over the miniature furnishings. Unlike the more familiar narrative roles, this incongruous image recalls no counterpart beyond the fiction at hand. Instead, the son's contrary feelings of guilt, sorrow, resentment, hostility, and love must animate this being.

The "I," therefore, is a mobile structure that personifies the son's desire both to repeat and to displace the father: "In the *other*," Jacques Ehrmann explains, "'I' sees the *same* as himself . . . and someone else besides him."[29] The identity of "I," already confused by the narrator's multiple roles, now ambiguously blurs with the third-person referent. Thus, "I" invents itself. Since this process of invention involves the participation of the author, the reader, and the first-person narrator, this strange "word-being" or "grammatical person"[30] may be occupied by any one of or all these participants at once, as they, too, merge with the "other."

"Daumier"

In "Florence Green Is 81," after the aging hostess announces her desire *"to go somewhere where everything is different,"* the narrator concludes, "A simple, perfect idea. The old babe demands nothing less than total otherness" (*CB*, 15). Unable to imagine such a journey, however, he ends his tale driving in circles of despair. Both, the character Daumier might say, are victims of the "insatiable" (*SS*, 214) self—Florence, erring by way of impossible expectations, complete abandonment of the world; the narrator, succumbing to the self's propaganda in worthlessness. Daumier's imposing list of self-analysis tomes suggests that the self is a ubiquitous, tyrannical scavenger: "The self is a dirty great villain, an interrupter of sleep, a deviler of awakeness, an intersubjective atrocity, a mouth, a maw" (*SS*, 219). Like Paul Klee, though, Daumier ignores threats to his well-being, beats his wings against the "cocoon of habituation which covers everything, if you let it" (*SS*, 227). He satisfies his yearning for "the other" by constructing surrogates engaged in brief, imaginary excursions: "The false selves in their clatter and boister and youthful brio will slay and bother and push out and put to all types of trouble the original, authentic self" (*SS*, 214).

In the story's design, perplexing headlines, rather than dots, herald clusters of shifting scenes and narrative viewpoints. A first-person Daumier opens the author's tale before unfolding his own. Despite his companion Amelia's skepticism, he has created a third-person Daumier, an antithesis to the "authentic self," a surrogate that is "in principle satiable" (*SS*, 215). The first-person Daumier can enjoy complete freedom in determining the heroic action that will merit his double's, and his own, measured happiness. Through the second scene's omniscient viewpoint, the reader then witnesses a miraculous feat: "In his mind's eye which was open for business at all times . . . in this useful eye," Daumier imagines "a situation" (*SS*, 215).

The "situation" is roughly a Zane Grey drama that flouts historical accuracy. Yet it is not a place where *everything* is different, for Daumier borrows his props and characters from the familiar world. Mr. Bellows and Mr. Hawkins, caricaturistic cowboy executives in an organization called the Traffic, guard a herd of au pair girls and rustle up chilidogs; Ignatius Loyola XVIII rustles the reluctant herd but cannot satisfy their hunger; the scout Daumier, theatrically summoned by a musketeer, clears up a scandal involving a queen, a cardinal, and a stolen necklace. The only hitch in this "simple, perfect" scheme is that after the third-person Daumier swoons at the sight of Celeste splashing nude in the river, the first-person Daumier yearns for her in his own life. To distract his longing, he then creates a less rapturous surrogate, a second-person Daumier, who can contemplate and temper his double's excesses.

While Daumier sketches the interior narrative, Barthelme designs the larger canvas. First, each scene's context validates in some ludic arrangement its caption's puzzled wording. The bold-faced list of Mr. Bellows, Mr. Hawkins, the Traffic, and chilidogs (*SS*, 215), for instance, participates in the third-person Daumier's tale, described with painterly allusions to spatial relationships and color. Both headlines and corresponding scenes then direct the eye—the reader's "useful eye"—to the canvas's other parts. Most significantly, the metaphorical "maw," imaged in the opening scene as a "great flaming mouth" (*SS*, 214), chews on numerous associations with the "insatiable" self. Midway through the fiction, Daumier resolves to stuff the dirty maw with "neutral or partially inert materials" (*SS*, 219). After the next headline immediately announces that these same "neutral or partially inert materials" will ford a river, Celeste objects to being herded into the noxious jaws of vipers, wriggling in the dirty flood. A worse risk, Daumier warns her, is Loyola, whose sermons cannot whet her appetite for chilidogs, a deficiency that later causes the au pair girls to moan. Through this last scene's transformations and innuendo, the stuffing of orifices smacks of sexual desire. The first-person Daumier sublimates his hunger in an afternoon revery, imagining a bustling street scene where he admires girls' buttocks, officers' "long shapely well-modeled nightsticks," and the bulging "tomato-muscle" (*SS*, 218) of an organic-vegetable vendor's wares. Imprecations, moans, and the rending of hair sweetly serenade the whole. Later, a similar vision of Celeste's legs, buttocks, and hair causes the third-person Daumier's ecstatic swoon and arouses the first-person Daumier's temporarily insatiable desire. Finally, however, the first-person Daumier is sated when Celeste miraculously steps from the surrogate's fiction into his kitchen. He prepares her a supermarket feast to celebrate their impending rite, but she rejects his Fritos and Tab. This is not food, Celeste complains, and begins the "cooking" herself.

Temporarily cheerful, Daumier wraps the surrogates and their cast in tissue and stores them in a drawer until some future unhappiness requires their diversions. Then, as he watches Celeste make a daube, he suddenly remarks that Amelia also makes a daube. To dwell on the difference between his romantic ideal and her mundane counterpart would surrender him once more to the insatiable self. Instead, therefore, he concentrates on his temporary pleasure. "The self cannot be escaped," he confides, "but it can be, with ingenuity and hard work, distracted" (*SS*, 230). Is the charming beauty in the kitchen really Celeste or plain Amelia seen with the first-person Daumier's "useful eye"? Either possibility is "a simple, perfect idea."

"Robert Kennedy Saved from Drowning"

Like Barthelme's phantom artist, whose amorphous balloon offers "the possibility, in its randomness, of mislocation of the self" (*SS*, 57), Daumier merrily calculates and shares his ego's distractions. Despite costume changes, both characters control their histrionics; play ends when they pack their props away. Fear, however, can dangerously accelerate and sustain the self's displacement. Catapulting from one identity to another, the desperate narrator/son of "Views" never concludes his dizzying charades. Similarly, in "Robert Kennedy Saved from Drowning," the personage "K.," a victim of his own identity's irreconcilable complexity, suffers chronic displacement. Like the Marivaudian being pondered near the story's end, K. is "a pastless futureless man, born anew at every instant" (*SS*, 85). Though these moments are all points of reference in K.'s life, truth and beauty dwell in the instant, not in a line.

The central character's abbreviated status (K.) ironically reflects this story's sketchy cameo of fame. Though K. is a public figure, dogged by aides, political colleagues, family, waiters, and reporters, no one— not even K. himself—really knows this enigmatic personage. As if to resolve his mystery, the text's fragments accumulate like leaves in a journalist's notebook, penned, it seems, by a relentless hound. Terse captions mark the narrative trail. Under "K. at His Desk," the narrator spins off metaphors to grasp K.'s extraordinary versatility with a common telephone—"a whip, a lash, but also a conduit for soothing words, a sink into which he can hurl gallons of syrup if it comes to that" (*SS*, 76). Under "Speaking to No One but Waiters, He—," the narrator dashes down K.'s exotic menu choices (perhaps K. is what he eats?). Narrowing aesthetic distance, the narrator also interviews K.'s familiars.

Several quoted fragments boast confidants' intimacy; however, these voices and their respective texts not only enhance K.'s mystery, but also harbor secret identities of their own. At best, a capital letter or a convenient pronoun locates a speaker. Secretaries "A" and "B," for instance, imbue K.'s behavior with symbolic import: K. is forgetful because he *wills* his mind free; K. personally delivers "get well" tulips because of his rare empathy. In later fragments, innuendo and ambiguous identities apparently encode ambivalence, fear, or threat. In "Karsh of Ottawa" (literally, an advertisement in the *New Yorker*), a quoted "I" recalls how "we" commissioned a sitting of K. Yet no mention of paint or photography verifies the plan's innocence. Instead, Karsh's preoccupation with when and where to perform the proposed "shot" ominously muddles the sitting's intent: "He said some people were very restless and that made it difficult to get just the right shot. He said there was one shot in each sitting that was, you know, the key shot, the right one" (*SS*, 79–80). A later passage echoes such nebulous communications. Under "K. Puzzled by His Children," the subject reads his weeping children a German picture book: "A ist der Affe, er isst mit der Pfote. (A is the Ape, he eats with his Paw.)" (*SS*, 81). The children, apparently estranged from their prodigal pa, continue to wail, while K. perseveres in frustration. Taken with several dream entries, this last passage complicates the narrator's identity as well.

In most fragments, a third-person objective narrator appears to record the observations, anecdotes, and quoted testimonials that explore K.'s life. But in two passages an "I" who is not displaced by quotation marks speaks directly from the text. Witnessing K. with his children, this voice first undermines its own findings: "I am a notoriously poor observer" (*SS*, 81). Thus, well into the story, "I" betokens a weak, unstable narrator. But in the last fragment, when K. thrashes helplessly in murky waters, "I" casts a line to save him from drowning: "I am on the bank, the rope wound round my waist, braced against a rock. . . . I pull him out of the water" (*SS*, 85). Jacques Ehrmann's comment that "in the *other*, 'I' sees the *same* as himself . . . and someone else besides him" once again illuminates the questionable identities of Barthelme's characters. Like "I," K. wavers between insecurity and confidence. In "K. on His Own Role," K. longs to sit alone in a garden, peacefully contemplating life's "small events" instead of wrangling with crises (*SS*, 83). However, monitoring life's small events is the narrator's task. K. then recalls his importance to "other people": "I have a responsibility . . . for the common good" (*SS*, 83). Yet the narrative "I" later takes responsibility for K. when the story's hero, after discarding his cape and sword on the bank, flounders in crisis.

Also disconcerting is the inexplicable ability of the narrator—this "I" or another elusive observer—to record dream content. In "Sleeping on the Stones of Unknown Towns (Rimbaud)," K. strolls the streets of a French or German city, the site strangely uncertain. "The shop signs," K. and the narrator note, "are in a language which alters when inspected closely, MÖBEL becoming MEUBLES for example, and the citizens mutter to themselves with dark virtuosity a mixture of languages" (*SS*, 78). This passage ultimately glosses all the story's ambiguities. Characters, setting, action, and viewpoint are, after all, the creations of language. If language "alters when inspected closely," so do its ostensible referents. As experience teaches Miss Mandible's middle-aged protégé, "signs are signs, and some of them are lies" (*SS*, 34). Therefore, neither K., the narrator, nor alleged events can be known. Inevitably, like the fiction's other constituents, K. "retains his mask" (*SS*, 85).

"The Captured Woman," "What to Do Next," and "Bone Bubbles"

Barthelme's dizzying play with narrative identities sometimes effaces characters entirely. The "I" then denotes an illusory grammatical structure glimpsed only through its various relationships with the text's other letters or words. Toying with "I" in "The Captured Woman," for instance, Barthelme substitutes capital letters for the story's participants, so that each of the text's voices—not just the first-person narrator's—is located by a single unit of speech. In one passage, Barthelme assimilates "I" into a list of 10 strategists, all intent on seducing the contemporary woman: "P. uses tranquilizing darts. . . . D. uses chess. . . . S. uses a spell inherited from his great-grandmother. . . . X. uses the Dionysiac frenzy. . . . I use Jack Daniel's" (*SS*, 288). In the last sentence, subject-verb agreement and lack of a period after the capital distinguish "I" as a grammatical being slightly different from its comrades; however, its vertical alignment *in the story* with nine other capital letters and the parallelism of "use" overshadow this discrepancy. "I" merely leads (and ends) the narrative choir. Understandably, the captured woman later giggles when "I" tapes an *X* on the floor to commemorate their lovemaking.

Collectively bound by their dubious quest, the letters merge into a composite character—a hapless knight, displaced from Arthurian legend into a world of unchivalrous deeds. A punning discussion between "I" and "M." about how to woo a disinterested captive indicates how the voice of each capital fuses into one bungling, quixotic personage:

> "Speak to her. Say this: My soul is soused, imparadised, imprisoned in my lady."
> "Where's that from?"
> "It's a quotation. Very powerful."
> "I'll try it. Soused, imprisoned, imparadised."
> "No. Imparadised, imprisoned. It actually sounds better the way you said it, though. Imparadised last." (*SS*, 290–91)

Such dialogue, unencumbered by specific speakers, soon constitutes whole stories for Barthelme. Here, however, the fragment sufficiently illustrates the elusive central character; in the context of these floating quotations, the first-person pronoun can designate either "I" or "M."

"What to Do Next" stretches Barthelme's narrative wordplay to greater metafictional extremes. An instruction list teeming with convoluted cross-references, the story promises readers a healthy recovery from any "desperate" situation: death of the family dog, fear of writing a will, failure to atone for divorce with true love, a thoroughly botched life.[31] Once again, displacement begins with the first-person narrator but rapidly entangles other indefinite pronouns in the web. "I" and "we" betoken the authoritative instructions, taken individually or collectively; "you," on the other hand, nabs and demeans everyone who reads the text. "You" is "a banged thumb," a bungling "wimp and a lame" (*A*, 86). The instructions insist that they are "crucial to giving your leaning personality the definition that it lamentably lacks" (*A*, 84). "You," moreover, cannot escape these tyrannical authorities: "We have therefore decided to make you *a part of the instructions themselves—* something other people must complete, or go through" (*A*, 86). Paradoxically, "you" becomes a part of "I" and "we"—the instructions/ instructors; in addition, "you" embraces not only "they" and "everyone" implied in the preceding passage, but also "he," "she," "him," and "her": "It is true that what she is saying doesn't interest you very much, but don't tell her (or, if you are a woman, him—the instructions are flexible, the instructions do not discriminate)" (*A*, 82–83). As the preceding statement suggests, these pronominal beings also ambiguously cross-reference with other words by way of linking verbs: "—she is interesting but false. (It is not true that she is interesting but it is true that she is false.)" (*A*, 83). Even the adventurous reader spins in the vertigo of words' equivocal relationships. The fiction's interior structure is thus patterned by neither the deceptive linear design of the instructions nor a reliable "I," but by complex wordplay among pronouns and referents. Ultimately, "I" and "you" exchange roles of triumph and dismay in the appropriate paradox that ends the story: "Your life is saved. Congratulations. I'm sorry" (*A*, 86).

Though hypothesis suggests that readers participate in stories like "What to Do Next," Barthelme knew well the pitfalls of freeing language from its familiar function of signifying people and objects. The convoluted references in "What to Do Next" strikingly resemble wordplay in "Bone Bubbles," a piece Barthelme had to defend even to his own editors. Its text rushes out in all directions with strings of mysteriously patterned words: "bins black and green seventh eighth rehearsal pings a bit fussy at times fair scattering grand and exciting world."[32] This thrilling freefall, speeded up by a flood of monosyllabic words, eliminates the possibility of affixing grammatical function, of forming and retaining logical word combinations, or of forcing the words to convey some predetermined significance.

Even if we slow down the text, as we might rerun a film in slow motion, assigning meaning is still an exercise in futility. Removed from the text, the configuration "bins black and green," for instance, is a sound enough image if "bins" are receptacles. But reading the same configuration aloud swiftly also conjures "beings" with slurred articulation and truncated spelling (like "damfino" in "Great Days" [*F*, 241]). So which image is correct, a dempster-dumpster or mottled aliens? To take this whimsy a bit further, when replaced in the text, either configuration must reshape itself to make sense with another word group. Thus, "green" may be joined with "seventh eighth" to suggest a golf course's flagged oases, or (the choice is arbitrary) the first configuration may be deserted entirely to rationalize the point of "seventh eighth rehearsal." Every line of "Bone Bubbles" perpetuates such enigmas and compels the reader to zigzag repeatedly through this inexhaustible text.

In our 1988 interview, Barthelme conceded that "Bone Bubbles" probably earned its metafictional tag because it *is* about the provocative power of language, words' peculiar jazzlike rhythms and "ineffable" meanings,[33] rather than a finite world of reference outside the fiction.

He was always dismayed, however, that such tags eschewed his moral-artistic purpose. "Art is not difficult because it wishes to be difficult," he wrote, "rather because it wishes to be art. However much the writer might long to be, in his work, simple, honest, straightforward, these virtues are no longer available to him. He discovers that in being simple, honest, straightforward, nothing much happens: he speaks the speakable, whereas we are looking for the as-yet unspeakable, the as-yet unspoken" (*N*, 42). Measured against reader reaction, Barthelme lamented, "Bone Bubbles" was a "failed experiment"; measured by his own artistic intent, however, it was a passionate success. Art, he insisted, must be provocative: "tear a mystery to tatters and you have tatters, not mystery" (*N*, 46).

Unlike "Bone Bubbles" and its frivolous companions, Barthelme's numerous dialogue stories enjoy a more faithful readership. Aside from "Kierkegaard Unfair to Schlegel," "The Explanation" (*CL*, 1970), and the women's voices in *The Dead Father* (1975), most of these dialogues were first collected in *Great Days* (1979) and *Sixty Stories* (1981). Barthelme liked the bare-bones structures in part for their artistic advantages. He compared their leanness to Giacometti's elongated, skeletal sculpture (Zeigler, 55), their suggestive juxtapositions to a pointillist's effects, and their "weirdly musical" rhythms to poetry (O'Hara, 197). But by 1980, Barthelme seemed more interested in his stories' emotional poignancy than technical innovation. Because the dialogues often expose such intimacies, several are considered with the next chapter's moral analyses.

A Disreputable Gallery: The Picture-Texts

Though dialogue stories figure prominently in his work since the late 1970s, Barthelme closeted his interest in picture-texts after critic Diane Johnson applauded their absence from *Great Days* (O'Hara, 208). Nevertheless, their structures illuminate rhythmic patterns common to much of his short fiction. Composed of both verbal and graphic fragments, these collages belong to an historical gallery of "speaking pictures."[34] The graphic configurations include images of classical sculpture, "photographs" of characters, illustrations from science and technical manuals, perspective drawings, and engravings of weeping heroines from turn-of-the-century novels. These pictures often converse with texts in familiar formats. "Brain Damage" imitates a sixteenth-century emblem piece; "Eugénie Grandet" parodies Balzac's illustrated novel; "The Expedition" narrates a photograph album junket; "The Dassaud Prize" and "A Nation of Wheels" recall revolutionary dada and surrealist collages. But unlike their earliest predecessors, Barthelme's bold juxtapositions of pictures and texts usually create disorienting exchanges. In sixteenth-century emblem poems, the meaning that links motto, picture, and text is implied in the pictorial details and explicitly stated in the poem's moral instruction. But neither systematic orders nor authoritative instructions about the world solace Barthelme's readers. Rather than "correct" the world's confusion by falsifying it in the still life of artifacts, Barthelme's collages diminish life's vagaries to an "ongoing low-grade mystery."[35]

To entice readers to assent to such disorder, Barthelme confiscates from the world images of common objects: tires, machines, buildings, ice cream cones, nuns, nudes, umbrellas, birds, babies, a volcano. Similar to René Magritte's process of "resemblance,"[36] he then pastes these shapes in unexpected proximity on the picture plane and overturns their predictability as artistic symbols. That the constitutive elements are quotidian, banal, and simplistic, therefore, is not incidental. They *must* be so for the perceiver to invest his trust before engaging in the larger design's abstract, associative patterns. A composition's "resemblance" to the world deceives the viewer into thinking that he can successfully categorize and interpret his perceptual experience, while the tenuous relationships among the graphic and verbal fragments, varied, repeated, and retracted, counter his ordering activity with disorientation. Thus, as John Leland notes, the "play space" of Barthelme's collage fiction is located "between the promise and the lie of signs."[37]

This paradox of false promises complicates correspondences within each story. Any connection between pictures and text registers suspicion. Conventionally, an imaged pose, frozen perhaps in an attitude of joy, despair, fear, or indifference, announces the presence of a character caught at some point on the plot's corresponding gridwork. But an ironic caption's flat or comic tone often undermines the significance of a Barthelme character's pose (Figure: A woman menacingly bends over her sleeping spouse and prepares to hammer a spike into his ear. Caption: "Scenes of domestic life were put in the show" [*F*, 138]). Barthelme's pictorial arrangements do not comply with any specific narrative order, but cohere instead through patterns of visual rhythms established by repeating and varying familiar images within the assemblage.

"A Nation of Wheels"

"A Nation of Wheels" (*GP*, 135–46) illustrates how visual rhythms created by the "regular recurrence of identical or similar features within a spatial or temporal field"[38] offer surrogate assurance of continuity, even while the same features contradict one another as signs. In this piece, 9 of the 12 figures repeat a tire image, superimposed with a variety of incongruously posed and proportioned beings and objects: a swooning heroine, a cityscape, a horn, an ice cream cone, Akron's Venus. The reader then fantasizes narratives even without the help of title or text.

At least half the figures suggest ludicrous metaphors for rampant technology. The first one initiates this visual motif. Here, an upright tire—a static image in itself—terrorizes a tiny nude woman, superimposed at the collage's foreground. Technology's abuses similarly inform the fifth figure, where an enormous tire—like the mutant tarantulas, apes, and prehistoric dinosaurs of science fiction films—looms over a cityscape, threatening to crush all in its path. The nude's fleeing posture also correlates with other personages apparently overrun by wheels. In the seventh figure, a Victorian victim (an engraving reused in "Brain Damage") weeps in despair, but the tire rests on its side like a cat studying its cornered prey. In contrast to this distraught heroine, the eighth figure's subject, épée in hand, gallantly lunges at two upright tires, as if to run them through between the treads. Another pair of pictures also creates comic exchanges. In the third figure, a man, standing with legs apart in an authoritative stance, sounds a hunting horn to rally the nation against the invasion threatened by the other pictures. However, the fourth figure undermines this urgency. Here, a similarly dressed man, standing at ease with legs together, plays a musical horn; the horn's bell is a tire. The repeated images, though they sustain no consistent meaning as signs in a related sequence, nevertheless tempt pattern and order.

"At the Tolstoy Museum"

In this story, pervasively ironic allusions between text and pictures replace narrative's temporal continuity. As 14 disconnected paragraphs catalogue "facts" about Tolstoy's life, his work, and the museum's architecture, nine "photographs" record biographical data, the content of the museum itself (portraits, stories, personal artifacts), and architectural equivalents of the museum. In their disordered spatial arrangements, however, texts seldom confirm, in either content or tone, the story of nearby plates.

Thematically, the fiction subverts Tolstoy's exaggerated veneration. According to the text, the shrine's visitors, awed or chastised by the writer's ubiquitous "moral authority" (*F*, 122), sob uncontrollably. Guards with buckets of handkerchiefs tend the weepers. The building's architecture, like a stack of three increasingly larger boxes, is similarly imposing. Looking down from the third level's glass floor "provides a 'floating' feeling. The entire building, viewed from the street, suggests that it is about to fall on you" (*F*, 122). Exposing the text's mock seriousness, though, pairs of pictures visually inflate Tolstoy's relics and contradict the reported mourning. First, twin full-page portraits stare accusingly from the fiction's entrance. Superimposed near the second, however, is a squat Napoleonic figure, his "little man" complex shamed under Tolstoy's glare. Also, in the third figure, dry-eyed visitors study Tolstoy's coat, almost the height and breadth of the room. But the fourth figure, "Tolstoy as a Youth," humorously mimics this image. Here, a youth dressed in an oversized, loose-fitting coat or vest clutches a wine glass in his right hand and dangles an open book from his left. The pose promises that the young Tolstoy, a scholar of some worth and sophistication, is destined for the grandeur memorialized in the elder Tolstoy's greatcoat. Thus, the fourth figure paradoxically foreshadows the third. However, the third paragraph's childish trivia diminishes both pictures' promises: "As a youth he shaved off his eyebrows, hoping they would grow back bushier" (*F*, 119).

In other pictures, Barthelme superimposes images to flout the illusion of systematic orders. Both "The Anna-Vronsky Pavilion" and the final museum plaza sketch adapt eighteenth-century drawings to this purpose. Each sketch is grounded in the restrictive policies of the perspective artist who attempts to stabilize the world in a network of lines, to cloak its ambiguities through imposition of the mathematical ideals of Pythagorean laws. But the pictures are flawed. In isolation, they are cold, mechanical, static—a deceptive portrayal of the world. Barthelme exposes the lie by unexpectedly superimposing incongruous images, fore or aft, on the picture planes. Upon the benign calm of his Romanesque pavilion, he pastes a distressed damsel, struggling in a dark man's villainous embrace. Upon the museum plaza drawing, he pastes a reduced negative image of the Tolstoy portrait, already viewed twice at the story's entrance and, again in reduced form, in a Siberian hunt portrait. Closing the fiction at the sketch's horizon, the negative image looms imperiously where the disappearing lines of perspective converge. This last plate comically links Tolstoy's "floating" image with the "floating narrator" who remarked about his giddiness on the museum's third floor.

The patterns of repetition, so visible in both "A Nation of Wheels" and "At the Tolstoy Museum," do not occur randomly. As these stories illustrate, the variously posed images often repeat in pairs. Intervening fragments then disrupt the configurations and initiate new clusters of associations before a familiar element recurs. This pattern is almost identical to the timing, placement, and hyperbole that endow the spatial arrangements of Barthelme's verbal structures with their comic rhythms. The following excerpt from "The Glass Mountain" reveals this syntactical construct:

> 64. My acquaintances moved among the fallen knights.
> 65. My acquaintances moved among the fallen knights, collecting rings, wallets, pocket watches, ladies' favors.
> 66. "Calm reigns in the country, thanks to the confident wisdom of everyone." (M. Pompidou)
> 67. The golden castle is guarded by a lean-headed eagle with blazing rubies for eyes.
> 68. I unstuck the lefthand plumber's friend, wondering if—
> 69. My acquaintances were prising out the gold teeth of not-yet-dead knights.
> 70. In the streets were people concealing their calm behind a facade of vague dread. (*SS*, 181)

Sentences 64 and 65 are paired, with the repeated element varied in the second sentence so that its tone mocks that of the first. Sentences 66 and 70 similarly repeat. Yet sentences 66, 67, and 68 also disrupt the first pattern with references to other loci of perspective—the eagle, the knight "stuck" to the mountain, the people in the streets—frequently repeated in the story's text. But with the ludicrous exaggerations of sentence 69, comic only in its interplay with sentences 64 and 65, the earlier configuration and its familiar elements unexpectedly leap back into focus. The familiar feature's recurrence momentarily illuminates the core sentence before the patterns shift their perspective once more.

This type of "fugal continuity" also structures Barthelme's graphic assemblages. In fact, the primary visual images in "At the Tolstoy Museum" occur at precisely the same intervals as the varied core sentence in "The Glass Mountain" excerpt, with comparable emphasis on the third instance. Identical portraits open the fiction, but the Napoleonic figure comically undermines seriousness in the second figure. The next three figures—a pair of which contains the "greatcoat" pun— then shift the focus of perspective away from the portraits to other provocative images in the collage assemblage. Similar to the repetitive elements in "The Glass Mountain," these pictures, too, may be cross-referenced with the text, with each other, or with the collage figures that follow to shape a number of simultaneous configurations. Quite unexpectedly, the Tolstoy portrait then reappears in the sixth figure, where its reduced image fits proportionately with the other Siberian tiger hunters. The "message" of the first two portraits, varied and con-tradicted, thus completes the familiar syntactical pattern (interval 1–2–6).

In a 1984 apotheosis to John Hawkes's genius, Barthelme marveled over his colleague's flawless sentences. Citing a paragon of these beau-ties, Barthelme noted, "The rhythms of the sentence are perfectly in place: two quick phrases, a long declamatory statement, a hesitation and another statement."[39] Such orchestrations, however varied, are also the marvel of Barthelme's own designs.

"The Flight of Pigeons from the Palace"

Despite strong visual patterns—three perspective drawings, two land eruptions, another set of twin portraits—the graphic assemblage in "Flight" would be almost impossible to rationalize without the context that embraces the "amazing Numbered Man," the "Sulking Lady," the "Father Concerned About His Liver," an explosion, a volcano, and a miscellany of "babies, boobies, sillies, simps" (*F*, 136). Originally ti-tled "The Show," the story is a fantasy for a public bored with la vie quotidienne. Artists expected to create "new wonders" (*F*, 140) every season stage this arena of stunts and surprises.

Though the first several passages and a few thereafter correspond explicitly to accompanying images, much of the text dissipates into catalogs, digressions, or ellipses, as captions appear and then dissolve in a flow of associations. Spatially balanced on one page, for instance, are three textual fragments and the image of a ballerina standing atop a trapeze. The trapeze's supporting wires, like parallel poles, extend diagonally to complement the passage's length. Recalling the fantasy's context hooks the reader into the first fragment: "In the summer of the show, grave robbers appeared in the show" (*F*, 135). Though the robbers' acts bear no resemblance to the nearby picture, the passage's sad tone ultimately does. This fragment's last line initiates the connection: "In the soft evening of the show, a troupe of agoutis performed tax evasion atop tall, swaying yellow poles. Before your eyes" (*F*, 135). As the audience's gaze imaginatively drifts to the top of the tent, the illusion blurs. "Before your eyes" is not a troupe of agoutis, but the trapeze artist, swinging high above the crowd. The illusion sweeps the reader into the second fragment. Now, with the trapeze artist in focus, the commentary diminishes to the barely articulated, lyric reminiscence of one onlooker:

> The trapeze artist with
> whom I had an understanding
> . . . The moment when she failed
> to catch me . . . (*F*, 135)

But after extending this sad revery, the last fragment recoups the third-person voice, and "we" again admire this beauty together "through heavy-lidded eyes" (*F*, 135). The repetition of "eyes" and the pronominal shift from "I" back to "we" completes this three-part passage. Vision then shifts to another catalog of acts.

One of the story's perspective drawings harbors similar intimacies. Unlike its two companions—pictures of open-air pavilions and ambulatories—this figure reveals an interior structure with vaulted openings on each of three visible walls. Superimposed on the drawing are two images: an anatomical study of a human liver, its parts lettered for precise identification; and the stern profile of a bald human head. A flagrant disregard for proportion ironically counters this austere visage. The liver study, though centered at the structure's foreground, is disturbingly large. Even more disconcerting, the monumental head, thrust through a vaulted opening, stares at the liver. The latter image recalls the bungling elder in "Views of My Father Weeping": "My father thrusts his hand through a window of the doll's house. His hand knocks over the doll's chair, knocks over the doll's chest of drawers, knocks over the doll's bed" (*SS*, 121–22). In "Views," oedipal concerns evoke the exaggerated father figure, his disorienting presence heightened and exaggerated by the narrator's remorse and guilt. This technique, similar to Magritte's exaggeration of objects in *Personal Values* (1952), also confirms anomalies in the "Flight" drawing: "I put my father in the show, with his cold eyes. His segment was called My Father Concerned About His Liver" (*F,* 137).

The static precision of systematic orders—expected in an illustrated story's correspondences, graphically construed in perspective drawings—here tenders defeat. Emotion, not reason, illuminates the story's contingent interior worlds.

"Brain Damage"

The most startling and complex intermedia composition, "Brain Damage" offers neither the temporal continuity suggested by Tolstoy's biography nor the fantasy circus tent of "Flight" to contain its sphinxes and hippogriffs. Its phenomena, instead, seem all too real, its features evidence that the fiction is the cause, the effect, the product, the very site of "brain damage": "This is the country of brain damage, this is the map of brain damage, these are the rivers of brain damage, and see, those lighted-up places are the airports of brain damage, where the damaged pilots land the big, damaged ships" (*CL,* 146). Swamped in this "gray area where nothing is done, really, but you vacillate for a while, thinking about it" (*CL,* 134), the reader slogs over ravaged terrain. Though no Virgilian guide safely pilots him through the slough, comic patterns of resemblance abate the pilgrim's terrors.

The third figure's familiarity illustrates the story's most obvious ruse. Closely resembling a picture from Geoffrey Whitney's *A Choice of Emblemes* (1586), Barthelme's figure depicts Zeus's notorious punishment of Prometheus for defying the Olympian ruler's iron will: bound by adamantine chains to a barren crag, Prometheus suffers a ravening eagle's relentless assault. In Whitney's image, an accompanying poem's didactic couplet explicitly confirms the emblem's moral: "That he, that still amid misfortunes stands, / Is sorrow's slave and bound in lasting bands" (Klonsky, 37). As the Elizabethan might expect, an orderly scheme of correspondences links motto, picture, and text, and instructs him in sin's harsh dues.

Barthelme, in contrast, flouts this scheme by adding three new participants and a mocking commentary. Two women—one battling the eagle, the other collapsed from her struggles—fittingly recall the exile's sympathizers. However, a boy at the foot of the barren crag—

now a mere rocky stub—ignores the drama unfolding just above him. Further disconcerted by the motto's incongruous headlines ("RHYTHMIC HANDCLAPPING / SLEEPING / WHAT RE-COURSE?" [*CL*, 138]), the reader searches the adjacent text for a meaningful explanation. Yet here he finds only a confessional litany of offenses, with none matching the heroic magnitude of Prometheus's error. A wayward journalist, the story's rebel has willfully "reported inaccurately," "misspelled names," "garbled figures," "put lies in the paper," "put private jokes in the paper," etc. (*CL*, 138). Reflecting the wages of ignorance or dementia, Barthelme's motto, picture, and text deflate the myth's dire lessons. Half-hearted guilt is just a pecking nuisance; the writer's tongue-in-cheek penance promises its own end-less tortures (no couplets stifle sin's boasts); and though the litany im-plies didactic instructions (don't mess with typeset; don't mess with management; don't mess with truth), the writer eschews authority's tenets ("guilty pleasures are the best").

Like so many Barthelme characters, the wayward journalist could plead "not my fault," for his damaged psyche lacks or misconstrues redeeming guidance. The story's "spirit teachers"—nuns, monks, a Mother Superior, an ESP counselor—promise "a rich new life of achievement, prosperity, and happiness" (*CL*, 133), but experience turns heads to the penny-ante rewards of fishing in the gutter. In one anecdote, nine waiters pass the buck—pass pennies, quarters, fives, tens, and a $50 war bond. In another anecdote, a great waiter earns cash and renown for swindling a wine novice. No tidy scheme ration-alizes the world's inequities or the soul's petty transgressions. Instead, teasing correspondences debunk absolute orders with nonsense. In the first figure, disembodied heads resting on blocks, their mouths agape, mime the blockheads duped into voicing the accompanying words:

CROWD NOISES
MURMURING
MURMURING
YAWNING

(*CL*, 135)

The text that follows memorializes the great waiter, who is ritually poached in wine and laid out on a bed of lettuce in the establishment where he had "placed his plates with legendary tact" (*CL*, 136). In the next picture, another disembodied head jokes that the waiter is now ready for the platter. Placed near its yawning orifice is a set of teeth—the waiter's "plates" perhaps.

Though brain damage ravages the story's landscape, humor and familiarity mitigate the populace's terror of affliction and encourage quests into the unknown. "Man likes signs and likes them clear," Barthes asserts,[40] but anchoring readers in simple, perfect orders betrays them to life's quagmires. According to Morse Peckham, "Art is the exposure to the tensions and problems of a false world so that man may endure exposing himself to the tensions and problems of the real world" (314). Assessing the disorienting snags in Joyce's tangled tapestries, Barthelme implicitly critiqued his own art, too: "The fabric falls apart, certainly, but where it hangs together we are privileged to encounter a world made new" (*AJ*, 14).

The Bean Waters of Babel

In his review of *Great Days* (1979), Raymond Carver worried that the book's disembodied, often nameless haunts never speak of "anything close or dear to the human heart." They just "babble."[41] Granted, the dialogue stories in particular lack a fleshy human presence, a complete gene package, narratively fed, perfumed, and attired. True, also, the soap opera of Hilda's futile social climbing—"On the Steps of the Conservatory" and its sequel "The Farewell"—seems to occasion only clever bantering. Yet it is almost impossible to separate the many tongues of Barthelme's fiction from the voices of his own time. Rhythms in "Sentence," "Aria," "A Manual for Sons," and "Critique de la Vie Quotidienne" churn with the emotional tides of their speakers. Human relationships—a morning embrace, the parental stranglehold, wedded hell—swirl in the maelstrom. Just as surely, Hilda's kin number not only TV's shallow idols, but also the ghostly millions who daily relinquish the risks and triumphs of individualism to hibernate in anonymity's snug cocoons, to petrify in stony institutions like government, religion, loveless marriage, boredom, old age. Hilda's melodrama or the Edward and Pia tales, Barthelme explained in our 1988 interview, create the "documentary effect" of "*cinema verité*, a film of these people's lives with the dull parts left in. In a sense," he concluded, "nobody's taking heroic action."

Contrary to Carver, Jerome Klinkowitz notes the value of Barthelme's story ethic: "His motive is journalistic; despite the fact that his subject is often the materiality of language, in Barthelme's hands it takes on satiric significance—making him one of the leading social reporters of his day, because in the media-conscious world of contemporary America so much reality *is* linguistic. Barthelme's innovations, therefore, may be less fictional than representatively historical."[42] Sometimes, as in "Sakrete," "The New Owner," and "Pepperoni," his stories seem only to exclaim evidence of the world's messiness—petty theft, greed, gratuitous journalism. But Barthelme contended that he also boobytraps his fiction with thousands of moral barbs, tiny thumbscrews, each given a hearty twist for "the Good" (Ziegler, 45–46).

Style, he said, allows writers to "quarrel with the world," yes, but it also inspires "alternative realities, other possibilities" (*N*, 50) to a fearful or passionless life. Hence, to quarrels with his method, his retort is decisive: "Bless Babel" (*N*, 49).

On the "warm tympanic page" (*SS*, 284), Barthelme wages political battles and exposes human frailties. But he also crusades for keeping faith in the prospects of mortal existence—like the writer's sentence, "a structure to be treasured for its weakness, as opposed to the strength of stones" (*F*, 163).

The Ironist's Quarrel with the World "Kierkegaard Unfair to Schlegel"

Barthelme never credited his stories with eliciting sweeping social change. Ambivalence, not humility, accounts for this disclaimer. Often, he nervously camouflages his stories' moral weaponry in undertone or defuses it with jokes. As "Kierkegaard Unfair to Schlegel" demonstrates, he doubted both the power and validity of the ironist's ploys, even though he admitted his own unavoidable complicity in such strategies. Leaping repeatedly from chair to couch in this psychoanalytical question-answer dialogue, Barthelme plays devil's advocate to his own devices to examine the ironist's dilemma.

According to Barthelme, the story opens with a masturbation scene, a man on a train using a shapely passenger for his narcissistic fantasies. The scene was intended to equate this detached, egoistic indulgence with the ironist's "subjective freedom" (*SS*, 164), a parallel that Barthelme suspected is lost on his readers (Ziegler, 46). The connection begins shortly after "A," the masturbator, confides this reminiscence to "Q," the analyst. When "Q" then suddenly questions "A's" political activity, the character echoes the author. Defending himself as a concerned, socially conscious citizen, "A" asserts that he marches to a democratic beat: "I make demands, sign newspaper advertisements, vote. I make small campaign contributions to the candidate of my choice and turn my irony against the others. But I accomplish nothing" (*SS*, 161). Yet in a humorous, even useful way, "A" scoffs, the government, the ultimate unintentional ironist, has subverted its own credibility by selling off surplus uniforms and unwittingly clothing a whole "clown army" (*SS*, 162) of funky little rebels with its mismatched rejects. Thus, like the masturbatory fantasy, irony's scores afford someone "a poor . . . a rather unsatisfactory" delight (*SS*, 167), however weakly aimed the missiles. In the analogy resides Barthelme's ambivalence about his own indulgence in such "guilty pleasures."

Still, "A" defends his motives and, in doing so, upholds Barthelme's strategies as well. He tells an anecdote about a family who has amassed an outrageous stock of games and toys. This compulsion for play seems to him an unhealthy symptom of acute "boredom" and the family's attempt to mask its "disease" (*SS*, 163). Absurd jokes about the problem expose the deceit, however, so that neither the family nor society can hide its folly in the closet with the pogo sticks and mallets. His irony, moreover, absolves him of the problem altogether. But does his irony recommend more responsible behavior? To "A's" chagrin, Kierkegaard says "no."

Kierkegaard, "A" and Barthelme complain (Ziegler, 47), ignores these little meliorative crusades and condemns all ironists as amoral annihilators. Disregarding truth, the ironist says what he does not mean. Worse, his jokes allow him to obliterate despicable situations or objects without replacing what he vanquishes. He becomes free at the world's expense. Even if, like Schlegel, he posits a new, perfect poetic order, Kierkegaard concludes, the discrepancy between the latter and its flawed predecessor only incites the hostility of the shamed victim. "A" resents this assessment of Schlegel and Kierkegaard's suggestion that, as an ironist, "A" himself has abandoned all moral responsibility to the world. Actually, the "disapproval" (*SS*, 166) of Kierkegaard and the equally intolerant analyst seems the more dangerous threat. The analyst's calculated superiority over "A," the imperfect but socially conscious citizen, demonstrates this conclusion. After seducing "A" into reluctantly stripping his ego, "Q" denies any responsibility for the betrayal—"I'm not your doctor" (*SS*, 167)—and then gloats over his prey's calamity: "Q: (aside): He has given away his gaiety, and now has nothing" (*SS*, 168). "Q" then, ironically, concludes the story with a mockery of "A's" masturbation anecdote. His ostensibly serious tale is about Pasteur. Under the pretense of soliciting a donation from a widow, Pasteur, "distracted, ashamed" (*SS*, 168), guiltily persists in his alleged efforts: "He becomes more firm, masters himself, speaks with force, yet he is not sure that she knows who he is, that he is Pasteur" (*SS*, 168). Like the man on the train, Pasteur seems anonymous, his motives undetected by the prey in his apparent fantasy, until the couple's inane weeping abruptly ends "Q's" villainous tale. This absurd incongruity exposes the analyst's joke as "Q's" disapproval of "A's" behavior. "A," as Kierkegaard predicted, acknowledges the assault "bitterly" (*SS*, 168). In the face of such threats, concludes the narrator of "Hiding Man," "there must be room for irony" (*CB*, 27).

In Barthelme's stories, human frailty certainly dulls the wits to countless abuses and seldom musters more than spasms under pressure. But these awkward heroics bear some characters through the wilds of mortal life. Their tales, therefore, never suggest that remote Edenic gardens are either feasible or even desirable (Kierkegaard's concept of irony presupposes this wish). More than 15 years after "Kierkegaard Unfair to Schlegel" first appeared in the *New Yorker*, Barthelme published another pseudopsychoanalytical dialogue. "Basil from Her Garden" updates the earlier story's ambivalence with the mature author's confidence in imagination's access to an imperfect world's riches.[43]

"Basil from Her Garden"

In yet another passage from "Kierkegaard Unfair to Schlegel," "A" confides an anxious dream about his father's disapproval. "Basil from Her Garden" not only opens with a similar dream, but also, like the earlier story, ponders the sources of human desire, guilt, and folly. "A," for instance, is not a dashing hero. He is just an "ordinary" (36) fellow with the usual photos, identification, and plastic in his wallet. But he frets about his "inadequacy" (37), notably in marriage. Instead of the "laughing cavalier" that his wife deserves, he is as often a "rank pig-footed belching blunderer" (38). Despite suffering guilt about disappointing his wife, he commits adultery with Althea. Like a ship's voyage on a vast, unrelieved sea, his passage from birth to death seems "slow" and "inexorable" (38). Contrary to "Kierkegaard," however, this story does not debate irony's role in these issues. Neither do "A" and "Q" engage in bitter rivalry. While the speakers do philosophize about ethics and human prospects, they take turns sharing, analyzing, and easing each other's worries.

The "mental exercise" (38) of this self-scrutiny ultimately reveals an inherent gift for transcending the common run: the human mind. A flicker from the "mind of God" (37), it casts its golden rays into the darkest holes of the mundane world. Like the black swarms of insects that briefly interrupt this meditation, life's mishaps cloud vision. Yet human reason withstands these little disturbances by rationalizing, if not fully understanding, their "fit" in the larger scheme of things—"fit in a stately or sometimes hectic dance with nonfit" (39). To the faithful, moreover, imagination restores passion and worth. Though "A" initially laments his "inadequacy" and dwindling prospects, for instance, his mental resources dispel the gloom. First, he reasons that the Seventh Commandment's prohibition of adultery is "wrong" (36). Logically speaking, "A" contends, would Christ visit other planets and repeat His trials for all lustful creatures (i.e., intelligent but horny "boll weevils" [37])? Would God waste His omniscience monitoring lecherous liaisons in every sleazy motel on Earth? More significantly, would God endow mankind with imagination's radiant visions and not expect him to covet such beauty? "A" thinks not. Any flaws in this logic he attributes to mankind's "imperfect" (37) understanding. God, too, loves irony.

Both "A" and "Q" illustrate the redeeming benefits of faith in these mental powers. With imagination's eye, for example, "A" sees the otherwise cool, "boring" (37) Althea as a seductive hothouse beauty. Particularly in the last decade of Barthelme's work, such spiritual enlightenment and physical desire almost invariably occur together. Imagination's reward, after all, is delight in the physical world. But "A" also explains that mortal joy is not limited to sexual desire. He and a neighbor share the pleasing rites of Platonic affection. He raises her car battery from the dead; "she gives [him] basil from her garden" (38). He covets this bond as certainly as he covets Althea.

Though "Q" more readily settles for "too little" (39), his companion's "mental exercise" inspires him to imagine greater possibilities as well. Buoyed by "A's" gathering faith, "Q" drifts into a heroic revery that scales knightly romance to "fit" an ordinary world. Instead of a white charger, he rides a truck; instead of a crest, he wears the logo of his trade. He is, ironically, an exterminator. With his lethal wand, he rids suburbia's castles of swarming pests, life's little disturbances. A grateful housewife chastely rewards his commendable deed. Approving the "appropriateness" (39) of "Q's" ennobling role, "A" now affirms the dialogue's moral: "Transcendence is possible. . . . Believe me" (39).

Especially during the Vietnam War years, stormy disturbances almost relentlessly obliterated the rays of such confident visions. "Let there be light!" was Barthelme's battle cry, but loyal troops were few. Framed by the perspectives of "Kierkegaard Unfair to Schlegel" and "Basil from Her Garden," however, the following analyses indicate that Barthelme eventually enlisted substantial visionary forces. Impervious to laggards and doubters, they march from dawn to death in the world's "most exquisite mysterious muck" (SS, 158).

"Me and Miss Mandible"

Since the 1960s, Barthelme's irony has targeted institutions that entrap unwary masses as surely as Thoreau's "sleepers" mortgaged their autonomy to industrialism. "Sentence" testifies that humanity's "ruling bodies" (*F*, 159), among whom rank the Board of Education's teaching armies, have fouled the "underground mental life of the collectivity" (*F*, 159) with error. Despite the risks of assailing these inexorable systems, an occasional heroic chump spills his "heart's blood" (*F*, 160) to spar with society's guard.

Joseph, the failing persona of "Me and Miss Mandible," suffers mishaps in marriage, the army, and an insurance career, when finally his compassion for a loss victim exposes his disloyalty to the corporate dollar. Thus, his disgruntled boss, possibly conspiring with Joseph's heartless wife, relocates "The Adjuster" (*SS*, 26) to the sixth grade. Here, students mechanically chant allegiance to the American flag and the absolute principles of mathematics. Here, authorities promise students the wisdom "to take the right steps and to obtain correct answers" (*SS*, 27) to life's problems. Having pointlessly whitewashed trees for the army and sorted through the debris of world calamities as a claims agent, Joseph, unlike his starry-eyed classmates, knows better than to accept such "outrageous assurances" (*SS*, 32) as trustworthy "signs" (*SS*, 33). Nevertheless, he does not warn the children that life's machinery malfunctions.

Like too many of his failing contemporaries, Joseph resigns himself to humanity's irrevocable folly. Demoralized by his tour in the world's trenches, Joseph now weakly abandons his previous ethic and seeks a safe, anonymous slot in the "common run" (*SS*, 33). Miss Mandible, whose "heart's blood" is probably not "of the first water" (*F*, 160), rejoices in his adjustment. The children, meanwhile, ignorantly await delivery of life's promises, never fully computing betrayal in Joseph's capitulation or the lies in scandal-sheet sagas. Miss Mandible's lusty cloakroom tryst with Joseph, in fact, excites hope in the children for similar prospects.

"The School"

Naïveté also muddles the villainy of signs in "The School," at once a much darker picture of formal education and a stronger statement of resistance. The system mandates class projects to teach children how to be "individually responsible" (*SS*, 309). The system does not, however, prepare the children for the only sure consequence of such an investment. As death claims the children's trees, snakes, gerbils, and classmates, the teacher desperately rationalizes the losses to quell rising fears. His superiors, on the other hand, make no excuses, never even comment on the disasters. Yet neither the teacher nor his charges accept religion's excuse for this wholesale slaughter. Consequently, the children clamor for an act of love—"an assertion of value" (*SS*, 312)—to rekindle their faith in life's scary enterprise.

The teacher takes the risk. Though not with the same fervor that Miss Mandible clenched Joseph, he defies school rules and modestly kisses his assistant, Helen. In both stories, love inspires independent action (Miss Mandible is "ruined but fulfilled" [*SS*, 35]). In "The School," it also encourages belief that "there [is] value everywhere" (*SS*, 312). As Mad Moll concludes in "The Emerald," desire of any degree—whether lust or chaste affection—is better than no desire at all. In Barthelme's stories, however, one can never be sure if love's vessel, once dipped in the font of joy, will not later be villainously laced with poison. Therein lies the risk.

"A City of Churches"

Echoing the schoolchildren's doubts about death's ticket to eternity, this story questions the paradoxical implications of religion. If God's order is perfect and absolute, why do so many dogmas vie for exclusive billing? How can the soul in service to rigid institutions be free?

Prester is a city of churches—*only* churches—hulking traditional units wedged next to bold modern structures. Held in thrall by these medieval offspring, the populace works and sleeps under their relentless scrutiny. On newcomers like Cecilia, their influence is also quick and subtle. Standing dumbstruck in a belfry apartment, Cecilia "involuntarily" invokes "God Almighty" (*SS*, 211). A Prester real-estate entrepreneur, Mr. Phillips, then tries to intimidate her into passively accepting her niche in the zombie citizenry.

But Cecilia is a self-reliant mortal, endowed with the fires of her own hopes. Her wish for her own dwelling apart from the churches wrinkles the city fathers' blueprint and challenges the validity of Prester's perfect order. While others sleep, moreover, Cecilia wills her own dreams, "mostly sexual things" (*SS*, 212). Here, again, desire fuels indepen-

dent action. Like Prometheus, she bucks the fiat of religious rational-
ism and threatens to dream "the Secret" (*SS*, 213)—the courage of free
will—that can topple Prester's thralldom.

These stories are not so much attacks on formal education and religion as alarms to rouse people from their complacency. For Barthelme,
the government posed the gravest dangers, and he frequently targeted
this institution's errors during the Vietnam War years. *Unspeakable Practices, Unnatural Acts* (1968) hosts his most explicit political fiction. "The
President," "Game," "Report," and even "The Indian Uprising" all
criticize military aggression and the communication failures that per-
petrate humanity's worst crimes. If "The Indian Uprising" buries its
street battles under barricade debris and swirling filaments of words,
the other three stories focus clearly on their targets. Only the habitual
jokes occasionally deflect Barthelme's missiles.

"The President"

Couched in melodrama, this story's satire disguises several historical
parallels. Similar to Charlie Chaplin's slapstick assault on Hitler in *The
Great Dictator* (1940), "The President" profiles a small, dark, rhetori-
cally charismatic politician. Apparently a warmonger scheming another
holocaust, the President addresses constituents in gripping but nebulous soliloquys. Worse, he broods on "the death theme" (*SS*, 60). Yet
awed by glory propaganda, desperate for leadership, or simply terror-
ized, citizens faint to avoid acknowledging awful truths.

Whereas Chaplin's film, breaking conventions, ends with the actor's
explicit plea for peace and sanity—a moral mandate that sent American
isolationists scurrying—Barthelme's finale does not risk such disturbing challenges. Punning on "pits," for instance, evades the horror of
mass graves, even though into these pits will apparently fall both
"sleepers"—citizens oblivious to pending doom—and projected war
dead. The punning begins in the story's opening paragraphs, where
the narrator recalls the President's jaunty campaign tune, "Struttin'
with Some Barbecue,"[44] and the tiny politician's appearance at *The
Gypsy Baron*. The story also ends at this performance. Ironically, the
mysterious President has by now enlisted all the populace as unwitting
actors in his own dark charade. Outside, a unit of mounted police
swoons "en bloc"; inside, a regiment of ushers, "enforcing silence"
(*SS*, 62), hushes the madly applauding audience. Finally, the opera's
cast slides "into the orchestra pit in a great, swooning mass. We

cheered," submits the narrator, "until the ushers tore up our tickets" (*SS*, 62).

If allowed to reign, "The President" warns, this sort of worldly specter will draw the final curtain on humanity.

"Game"

The characters in "Game" dramatize a more potent story of military sabotage and psychological intrigue. "Owing to an oversight" (*SS*, 64) by their superiors, the narrator mechanically repeats, he and Captain Shotwell have been confined to a dank underground shelter for over 100 days. Secrecy not only encodes their ostensible task, but also obscures communication. If "certain events" occur on the "console" that they monitor, they must turn their "keys" in specific "locks" to activate the "bird" (*SS*, 63). Trapped in this green concrete limbo, however, they are no longer "sure what is oversight, what is plan" (*SS*, 65). Waiting, uncertainty, and ambiguous signs breed distrust. Each officer hides weapons to shoot the other if "strange" (*SS*, 64) behavior warrants attack, but neither knows anymore what "strange" means.

The mission is a nightmare in both its suggestion of nuclear holocaust (the narrator and Shotwell may be the only survivors) and embedded dream imagery. The latter plays on the oblique symbolism of words and actions. As time's suspension blurs the threshold between waking and sleeping, confinement's haunts pervert desire. Shotwell plays alone with his jacks, bouncing his rubber ball "in a steady, stolid, rhythmical manner" (*SS*, 67). Though the narrator covets Shotwell's diversion, the captain denies the narrator's requests to play "twosies," and locks the jacks and ball in his attaché case. The narrator then counters this strange "jacks-behavior" with peculiar "writing-behavior" (*SS*, 66). Distracting his thwarted lust, he uses a diamond solitaire to scratch "descriptions of natural forms on the walls" (*SS*, 66), ironically including a baseball bat in the list. If dream imagery, this action may be rationalized as loneliness for his estranged Lucy, and the bat as a spontaneous association of the diamond with a baseball field. However, after he obsesses to 4500 words on the bat's phallic shape, length, and comfortable "handhold" (*SS*, 66), he concludes, "I am not well. . . . I am aching to get my hands on the ball, on the jacks" (*SS*, 67).

Even when fear ultimately chases sleep, the narrator and Shotwell veil their needs in the mission's jargon. Too terrified to speak directly about the gross error that their abandonment implies, they "console" each other, whispering intimacies in the code of "keys" and "locks."

"Report"

In 1968, Barthelme idealistically hoped that "Report" would effect a ceasefire to the Vietnam conflict (Ziegler, 44). To this end, the story's persona, an emissary for antiwar protestors, tries to reason with the chief war engineer in the bluntest terms: "The war [is] wrong"; "large countries should not burn down small countries"; the government's senseless, deadly "errors" must be stopped (*SS*, 87).

But common sense never sways a Frankenstein mentality, so, once again, faulty communication aborts a persona's mission. First, the chief muddles the issues by defending the engineers' ingenious work—"evaporated thin-film metallurgy," "gross interfaced space gropes" (*SS*, 87)—with technological gibberish. He then misconstrues the emissary's motives as an "ineffectual" lobbyist's "hatred and jealousy" (*SS*, 88). Most importantly, he cannot compute the logic of human ethics. Even though he boasts a sophisticated *"moral sense"* preserved on "punched cards" (*SS*, 90), he mechanically wills power and destruction. The war program, he insists, functions only on winning; stopping it would admit defeat. Furthermore, his war engineers have stockpiled indomitable weaponry: a "pufferfish toxin which precipitates an identity crisis," "the deadly testicle-destroying telegram," "a secret word," whose utterance "produces multiple fractures in all living things" (*SS*, 89). Though the chief insists that the "moral sense" will ensure mankind's safety from calculated extinction, the engineers already suffer compound fractures because of one colleague's egotistical blunder—"Some damned fool couldn't keep his mouth shut" (*SS*, 89).

This last line's joke is funny, but quips and Chaplinesque caricatures deprive some of Barthelme's fiction of whatever urgency was intended. In "Margins," the complaint that the government will not give the black demonstrator Carl a "cotton pickin' job" (*SS*, 12) similarly weakens the story's pervasive focus on racial stereotypes, even if Barthelme also implies that Carl should not expect any "givens." Laughter assuages rather than piques outrage. On the other hand, the explicit attack on military subterfuge in "The Mothball Fleet" is really no more incendiary. Looking back in 1988, Barthelme faulted this "butterfly effect" of his political protests. Perhaps, he suggested, he should have stormed the White House lawn in the company of Grace Paley.

Family Matters
"Critique de la Vie Quotidienne"

The only institution in Barthelme's stories to rival the government's arsenals and faulty wiring is marriage. Conspiracy lurks in the connubial cocoon, but it is also the sanctuary of love. Little wonder, then, that characters are perpetually caught in the crossfire of wrath's thunderbolts and desire's arrows, with men tallying a disproportionate number of wounds. Regardless of battle scars, the men are suckers for love. The promise of a beautiful leg or thigh lures them recklessly into the fray. As illustrated earlier, desire is perhaps mankind's only gift from the gods, but when the fire cools, malice kicks the ashes. Aside from a war of wits, Barthelme's couples seldom share themselves intellectually, so without the joys of sex, the wedded pair squares off. To the rivalry of the sexes, Barthelme hoists the balloon of the misbegotten.

Romance's "balloon goes up" (*F*, 65), explains the A&P checker in "Jaws," with the slightest breeze—a lingering gaze over the frozen foods, a duct tape flirtation. Battered by ill winds, though, it buries its riders in the deflated wreckage. In "Critique," several vignettes, like yellowed photographs from a dusty album, record the disappointments and fears that have thus dismantled an ordinary marriage. Weary of her domestic roles, Wanda sighs over the enchanting tableaus of romance and wealth in *Elle*, while her husband, the narrator, grows bitter from neglect or abuse because his family insinuates that he has intentionally subjected them to penury. Only one memory portrays him basking in their contentment—the night he fixed the wobbly seat on his child's "cheap bicycle" (*SS*, 188). More often, la vie quotidienne is a war zone.

God's and Wanda's retribution visits the narrator chiefly in the couple's only child. It urinates in the hotel bed that it shares with its parents, and it toasts death masks on the apartment radiator. If the bedwetting strategy enrages the father, the masks terrorize him. To his interrogation about their significance, the prophetic child replies, "Intimations of mortality" (*SS*, 187). Even the father's nine evening sloshes of J & B cannot defray such assaults. However, the child's most notorious harrassment occurs early in the story, when the imp demands a horse. Despite its vendettas, the scene is uproariously funny: a rocking chair captain reeling from his "six-o'clock equilibrium" (*SS*, 184) as each J & B soldier topples; a stubby brat punctuating its unreasonable demands with little hand chops. As the text and, indeed, the marriage cloth swiftly unravel, the family plummets from its precipitous balance.

In his rationale against buying his child a horse, the frustrated narrator couches a parable of his own capture and subsequent unhappiness. A horse longs to "roam, and graze, and copulate with other attractive horses" (*SS*, 184) in spacious climes; stifled in "a broken-down brownstone apartment" (*SS*, 184), the brooding animal will muss the bed, vomit on the floor, and even bash walls in his wrath. Unmoved, the brat ignores the lesson: his friend Otto has a horse, stabled for no small fee in a park meadow by the lucky youth's doting parents. Bitter over the financial inequities that this comparison conjures, the father now curses Otto's parents with stock market ruin, lurches for his last two drinks, and blasphemes his silent wife for delivering him this tiny outrage. She coolly retaliates by flaunting her lovely legs, "those legs you could have, if you were good" (*SS*, 185), and slinging dinner on the kitchen floor, where the pitiful narrator then skids on pork and *sauce diable*. Too broke or impotent for a rout at the bordello, the defeated narrator, armed with two extra drinks, finally resigns himself to sowing barley in the fallow fields of his " 'living' room" (*SS*, 186).

The horse parable and the family's distorted communication do not end here. After the divorce, Wanda visits the narrator's bachelor quarters, where the couple's string of toasts digresses into hostilities worse than any suffered on marital ground. Like Ahab swilling to the death of Moby-Dick, Wanda raises a sinister alleluia—"Health to the dead!"—and tries to shoot her former spouse with a "horse pistol" (*SS*, 189). But the misguided bullet destroys only a bottle of Scotch. Escaping this scene's "intimations of mortality," the narrator seeks courage in his eternal elixir. Assured a constant supply of J & B, he concludes the tale with a pun that flouts his near-miss with death: "There is," he asserts, "no immediate danger of a dearth" (*SS*, 190).

In light of Wanda's and earlier conspiracies, the reader's sympathy for wounded family members is as fickle as the characters' loyalties from one vignette to the next. Does the child wet spontaneously because of previous abuse or use its youth to veil malice? Does the saintly wife cower under epithets or feed her husband's ghosts with disappointment and contempt? The narrator certainly deserves some compassion, yet, alcoholism aside, he nourishes his own demons. He estranges himself from the child: " 'Your father is telling you to wash your face,' I said, locating myself in the abstract where I was more comfortable" (*SS*, 187). In his wrath, he even invokes destruction: "Is there to be no end to this *family life?"* (*SS*, 186). The reader yells for first one side and then the other in this tug-of-love.

The story tackles some scary social issues, yet invites repeated readings because Barthelme masterfully sustains tension between its cartoon violence and evening-news reality. While the text's undertow sweeps the reader into its growing tide, humor checks his impulse to paddle to fairer shores. The really scary part is that the family's abuses are so ordinary—exaggerated for effect but still ordinary. In "Affection," the "reader and advisor" Madam Olympia exclaims that she is "bored to tears" with these predictable tales of marital destruction, "to tears to tears to tears" (*F*, 72). Barthelme's reader, too, yawns at Claire's and Harris's initial lamentations. So midway through the story, Barthelme embellishes the couple's weary relationship, first with tabloid titillations and then with ludicrous soap-opera complexities. Give the public what sells. Like Harris, though, this same public denies real social dilemmas. *"The New York Times* will be published every day," he drones, "and I will have to wash it off my hands when I have finished reading it, every day" (*F*, 76). The marital violence in "Critique" and "Jaws," on the other hand, uproots indifference and protests, *"Wake up! Remember!"* (*F*, 66).

"A Manual for Sons"

No less treacherous than the chicanery of "wife-signs" (*SS*, 33) is the feigned innocence of Barthelme's men, particularly fathers. In "Grandmother's House," wistful male characters marvel over the feminine mystique: the ambiguity that underlies women's "cold moves" and "cozy moves" (*SS*, 452). Yet these middle-aged cronies disguise similar contradictions. Though they fret that wolfish young motorcyclists are stalking their daughters, they themselves long to nibble on forest nymphs. The men remember well their own reckless teens but paradoxically dissociate themselves from seductive wiles if the prey are not their own offspring. Recalling the emotional posturing in "Views of My Father Weeping," "A Manual for Sons" forges the father from a crucible of love and hate.[45]

A text dense with archetypal sires feverishly records the ubiquitous father's dissembling poses, hues, and tongues. The more determined the effort to humble this protean giant, however, the more godlike he looms. From his heavy baggage, the father doles mystic instruction—"the true and not-true" (*SS*, 251)—but mostly he dispenses fear. In his ascendancy, he throttles the egos of potential usurpers. Voice A, for instance, sadistically prepares his terrified child for the killing fields of school: "They going to vamp on you at that school, kid. They going to tear up your ass. . . . Your mother and I could socialize you here at home but it would be too painful for your mother and I who love you" (*SS*, 255). In his continuous barrage of rednecked effronteries against race, religion, and "dumb-ass women" waving harbingers of "the wrath to come," voice B likewise turns father-son ventures into brutal assaults: "C'mon kid, I'll let you hold the level. And this time I want you to hold the fucking thing straight. I want you to hold it straight. It ain't difficult, any idiot can do it. A nigger can do it. . . . HOLD IT STILL DAMN IT. . . . How come you're tremblin'?" (*SS*, 257–58). Similarly berated by the relentless interrogations of voice C, another son sublimates his fear, anger, and guilt in open masturbation. Hoping to escape "the wrath to come," he then repents his sins by obsessively washing his hands and banging his head.

The father will swallow his children or plump them up with love and later sell them to "bone factories" (*SS*, 254). Tyranny, however, is his only weapon against mortality. Despite his abuses, he inspires sorrow when insanity ushers him down the boulevards, stringing tin cans and crimson spittle, or his future lies behind him in a trail of "pathetic small hops" (*SS*, 253). Finally, the despot topples. Hair and jowls flapping in the upward gust, the "falling father" desperately recalculates his errors; hard work, he rationalizes, will reverse this accursed "downturn" (*SS*, 265). But time and gravity hold sway. Though the son may wish to rejoice in this windfall, he cannot, for even in death, the father—"an inner voice commanding, haranguing, yes-ing and no-ing" (*SS*, 270)—claims his bloodright. His identity bound to "the other," the son cannot renounce the paternal legacy, but he can attenuate the "enormities" of the father by becoming "a paler, weaker version of him. . . . thus moving toward a golden age of decency, quiet, and calmed fevers" (*SS*, 271).

"Chablis"

In two lighter stories, at least, fathers heed the omens tendered in "A Manual for Sons." Angry that his toddler is ripping pages from books, the rigid parent in "The first thing the baby did wrong . . ." (later, "The Baby") believes that he can correct this refractory behavior by incarcerating the little vandal for hours, even days. But finally admitting to the injustice of his inflexible laws, he modifies the ruling and rejoices in sharing the child's delinquency. "Chablis" similarly diminishes the tyrant's "enormities." Here, love not only motivates the compromise, but also eases the dread of mortality's dues—a frequent theme in the last decade of Barthelme's work.

Like the rest of his fraternity, the husband/father resents his ostracism from the family fold, in this case, the happy coterie of his wife and two-year-old daughter. Nevertheless, nothing in this story is truly on the rocks except his morning splash of chablis. With shameless pride, he catalogs the baby's irresistible charms. But when he sweetly asks the tot if she is "Daddy's girl," the churlish imp parrots "'Momma,' and she doesn't just say it once," he rails in his rejection, "she says it repeatedly, 'Momma momma momma'" (*F*, 11). Loyal to her own sorority, the wife, intent on having a Cairn terrier, manipulates her spouse's desire to gain the baby's favor. Though the child spouts only a four-word vocabulary, her mother insists that the daughter has eloquently requested the dog.

The narrator protests this entrapment and defends his right to deny the request. In the midst of silly excuses, he then suddenly betrays the real reason for his misgivings: "What's that baby going to do with that dog that it can't do with me? Romp? I can romp" (*F*, 12). Contrary to those fellows who long to flee the nest at the threat of the first strong gale, this father wishes only to shore it up. Out of devotion, he obsesses over his child's safety. He frets that her innocent curiosity will prompt her to taste-test a "diseased feather" (*F*, 12) or "jam a kitchen knife into an electrical outlet" (*F*, 13) or feast on toxic Crayolas. While he hovers over the paths of her perilous sojourns through the apartment and playground, the reader senses his struggle to spare authority's iron hand and allow her to sally forth freely, as she will someday have to stride into the world. Unlike a parent in "Rif," who will confidently teach her daughter to look just one direction as she crosses streets, he has not yet mastered this compromise. The narrator must first recognize in the child's dauntless spirit the flicker of his own indomitable youth.

The effects of ostracism help define this paradoxical interchange of parent/child roles and ultimately comfort the father. Near the story's opening, the narrator recalls his long history as a "black sheep" (*F*, 11). Unlike his wife and child, for instance, he has never deferred to the hypocrisies of religion (the baby abandoned the Baptists' daycare program for the Presbyterians' superior play equipment). In his youth, he and his brothers took turns enjoying the infamy of such independence. But as each one aged and accepted the responsibilities of job, marriage, and fatherhood, his wool became "grayer" and then entirely "white" (*F*, 12). At some point in the metamorphosis, the narrator also traded courage for fear. Hence, he ironically abhors his current "black sheep" status until he remembers the coup of his bold youth, in which he deftly veered from a head-on collision and strode away from death. "That was when I was a black sheep," he muses. "That was skillfully done, I think. I get up, congratulate myself in memory, and go in to look at the baby" (*F*, 13). Though he cannot check the father's compulsion to protect the child, neither can his love deny her an innocent's dream of immortality.

Mortal Visions
"Visitors"

In 1981, when Barthelme turned 50, he seemed pleased with the view from this lookout. The years, he said, had tempered his anger over humanity's folly and taught him to "cherish" life more and more as there is "less and less time" (Brans, 131). The implications of mortality, however, preoccupy Barthelme's last decade of stories, as aging characters debate, deny, or crusade for their remaining prospects. Not surprisingly, *gray* often betokens their uncertain status. Depending on a character's perspective, for instance, gray hair is either the gloomy wreath of death or the respectable laurels of experience. Though Bishop, the 49-year-old protagonist of "Visitors," still idles in the holding tank of middle age, he is beginning to feel the pinch of a silver crown.

Vulnerable to affection, understandably perplexed by the contradictions of age, Bishop never hides his humanity in caricature as so many other characters do. In fact, his story is among the least inventive but most candidly emotional of Barthelme's work. Bishop's cassoulet seduction of young, tanned Christie and particularly his hip bedtime art lecture to 15-year-old daughter Katie deliver the verbal gymnastics that Barthelme aficionados expect of the author's prose: "You get Kandinsky, a bad mother, all them pick-up-sticks pictures, you get my man Mondrian, he's the one with the rectangles and shit, . . . you get Moholy-Nagy, he did all the plastic thingummies and shit'" (*F*, 113).

However, Bishop's emotions—loneliness, desire, compassion—always simmer near the surface. This emotional complex gathers force in Bishop's tender relationship with Katie, who has been visiting her father each summer since her parents' divorce. As she languishes on the couch with stomach flu, he tries to cheer and comfort her, even though he, too, is ill. Other Barthelme men bemoan such imposition, but Bishop ministers to the task lovingly. His only complaint about the child is the joke he repeatedly musters to reconcile himself to divorce from Katie's "otherwise very sensible, and thrifty" (*F*, 109) mother. "'It was your fault,'" he teases Katie. "'Yours. You made too much noise, as a kid, I couldn't work.' His ex-wife had once told Katie this as an explanation for the divorce, and he'll repeat it until its untruth is marble, a monument" (*F*, 108).

The father-daughter confinement occasions not only intermittent conversations, but also drifting reveries that expose Bishop's disorienting status. Worried about his solitude, Katie encourages her father to live a little: "You could find somebody. You're handsome for your age. . . . You don't try" (*F*, 107). But this accusation is not quite true. As Bishop recalls, he has ventured into the city streets, only to be confused by the uncertainty of signs—the motley throng on West Broadway, artistic conspiracies. Once, he forced himself to enter a gallery and to wham "EVERLAST heavy bags" (*F*, 109) at the artist's invitation. He hurt himself. Similarly, though he picks up Christie on the street and lures her back to his apartment, their dialogue only underscores the disparity in their ages and interests. He babbles excitedly about Richard Widmark's "resilience" (*F*, 111), but she misses any hinted comparisons to Bishop. When she then extols Robert Redford, Bishop worries that "the conversation has strayed, like a bad cow, from the proper path" (*F*, 112). Even Katie is a paradox. Ill, she seems just a helpless child, but when Bishop is with her in public, he is self-conscious of her maturing body and their impression on strangers as she clings to his arm.

The story closes with Bishop pondering yet another, perhaps prophetic enigma: whether his elderly neighbors eat "breakfast by candlelight" because "they are terminally romantic" or because "they're trying to save electricity" (*F*, 114). Bishop is equally vague about his own circumstances. Resilience is an effort, but desire and romance are not dead in him. Unlike Barthelme's more pitiable characters, he has yet to witness or experience the paralyzing fear of the unknown.

"Morning"

This story's characters, in contrast, feverishly debate the implications of their mortality in a stark dialogue, stripped of the comfortable setting and explicitly identified characters and relationships offered in "Visitors." Distractions of style aside, "Morning" exposes emotions as honest and disarming as Bishop's. Hastening to remove from the world their worst fears, the speakers challenge each other to list their particular demons—sirens, vestments, breaking glass, an aging hand, but not death, not death, one thinly protests. As the companions alternately beat their oars against mortality's tide, acceptance and denial of life's inevitable end reciprocate. "Say you're frightened" (*SS*, 359), the first voice insists, at least twice repeating this plea. Initially more vulnerable than his companion, he pules about an enshrouding "gray light," while the other obliviously basks in his own brilliant orange desire, "a firestorm of porn" (*SS*, 359), the hoped-for glow beneath a girl's tight pants.

The conversation's nameless voices, abrupt shifts, and vague pronoun antecedents (especially the occasional "she") confuse the speakers' gender and number. Hence, if the text's marginal dashes punctuate shifts in *thought*, not necessarily changes of speaker, then one, two, or several characters may contribute ideas to, say, the "not afraid of" (*SS*, 360) litany early in the story. Even if, in the simplest reading, the marginal dashes designate two characters' alternating responses (voice A, voice B), the respective trumpets of terror and courage interchange midway through the dialogue. Forgetting his earlier advice that one should not stop long enough to dwell on his fears, the initially more confident speaker of this reading confesses his dread of mornings, weighty with a day's demands. The topic suddenly turns to death, and its lingering denial further undermines confidence. However, as the now-timid voice nervously elicits his companion's confessions to dread, the latter rejuvenates himself with romantic memories and a healthy list of his life's remaining prospects. True, morning confers upon the coward the terrifying responsibility of efficient and timely fulfillment of his prospects, of accounting to his conscience or spouse for some 480 meaningful daylight minutes. But chasing the night's phantoms, morning also ushers in hope. Though he cannot escape his mortality, he does not yet have to forfeit the delights of a "bright glorious day" (*SS*, 362) and consign himself to a dim room with lonely old men. He and his companion can enjoy the mottled hues of their metamorphosis, gray tendering orange, at least until "darkness, and they give up the search" (*SS*, 363). Regardless of the number or sequence of characters' voices, this debate's outcome is the same.

In the similarly affirmative dialogue "Great Days," a voice proclaims, "Each great day is itself, with its own war machines, rattles, and green lords" (*F*, 242), certainly an ambiguous offering. But as the story's closing knock-knock joke warns, only solitude and anonymity befall those who abandon effort, vigilance, and faith.

"The New Music"

Such hopelessness ultimately tolls doom for the lost, aging souls of "The New Music." Like the impotent cronies in "Grandmother's House," the speakers could initially be comics Tim Conway and Don Knotts lamenting the injustice of physiques out of sync with desire. Contrary to Arte Johnson's dauntless shuffling lecher on television's "Laugh-In," they suffer permanent losses with each new rejection. Youth mercilessly lords over its elders. One man recalls how a lovely young seductress, merely "practicing" her wiles, left him emotionally bankrupt, "like Insufficient Funds" (*SS*, 338). However, this defeat is only a prelude to the story's real subject: willful submission to death in life.

The man errs by denying himself any prospects beyond the virility and confidence of youth. With his companion, he compulsively defends himself as "a slightly old young man still advertising in the trees and rivers for a mate" (*SS*, 338), but his nervous jokes soon dissipate. No silver trophies immortalize his vital past, and, contrary to the popular adage, cleanliness—the virtue of his middle age—is far overrated. His more enterprising friend tries to allay these misgivings by proposing a special journey. Life's rapturous tunes, distant and strange, waft from Pool, a mecca of hope. There they can once again dance with young women and revel in "the new music." But distrust tarnishes the bright city's treasures. The demoralized speaker dismisses his friend's enticing descriptions as propaganda for a retirement compound or death camp, whose circuses, rich gardens, and grand estates merely distract attention from the truth: widows water lawns in solitude; photographs replace families in the retirees' homes; inmates receive little medals for daily survival; corpses grace the museum walls. The doubter makes excuses. He must tend to a shirt button, his camping gear, his prescriptive daily tasks.

Behind his paralytic fear looms the doubter's mother. Though only a dark memory, she is one of the few female progenitors in Barthelme's stories not seen chiefly in dubious battle with her spouse. Similar to the mysterious masculine authority in "A Manual for Sons," this mother is a soul-basher. Or so she seems. The spineless son recalls her ecstatic devotion to "the Eleusinian mysteries and the art of love" (*SS*, 343). Cloaked in secrecy, these ancient fertility rites venerated Demeter, earth mother and goddess of grain. In autumnal celebrations, when the corn was sown, a priestess coupled with her king on the ploughed earth to recapitulate Demeter's cornfield affair with Iasius and ensure a bountiful harvest. In other rites, Demeter's initiates manipulated phallic objects to reenact the immortals' copulation. Thus, the goddess's fecundity represented life's renewal for both the earth and mankind's spirit.[46]

In Barthelme's story, however, all these mythical elements compete with archetypal demons and desires in the mother-son relationship. Nightmarish visions conjure residual images of drunken orgies and bloody sacrifices to the ancient matriarch. A grim reaper, the heartless mother seems to conceive her fruits only to harvest and chop them up. The son manifests his ambivalence in a dream about a monster with Teflon claws. The monster complains that the "Curator of Archetypes" has been criticizing the beast for "shuckin' and jivin'" instead of "attacking, attacking, attacking" (*SS*, 345). Talk of "shuckin'" abruptly evokes the monster's demands for return of a cornflake. In other memories, the son perverts the ancient fertility rites and implicates his mother in his own maturing sexuality. On an autumnal walk, he dreamily relates, he once observed lovers couple "in the bare brown cut fields" (*SS*, 344) to his right; in the field to his left, however, rocked his stern mother, ignoring his polite tip of his hat to her: "She was pondering. 'The goddess Demeter's anguish for all her children's mortality'" (*SS*, 344). He then obscures the forbidden relationship in his insistence that "Momma wouldn't have 'lowed" (*SS*, 346) "the new music," but she loved lutes. They used to spend hours, the son recalls, "banging away at [their] lutes" (*SS*, 345).

In Demeter's rites of death and rebirth, the ceremonies, performed with music and dancing, symbolically delivered participants from mortal terrors into the divinities' glorious climes. Pool boasts not only these revelries, but also buildings and gardens splashed with red, Persephone's color, the hue of resurrection. Though eating the scarlet pomegranate relegated her to Hades for a season, Persephone, like the sown seeds, repeatedly rose from the realm of death to walk the green earth. Associating Pool's revelries with the taboos of his ambivalent relationship with his mother, the son chooses to decay in his current dormancy rather than risk the city's sure debaucheries and villainy. Like those "uninitiated" into the ancient mysteries, he is fated to grovel "in filth and fog, abiding in . . . miseries through fear of death and lack of faith" (Themistius quoted in Grant, 133). He submits himself to the stony crypt of death in life.

"The Emerald"

Barthelme lamented such hopeless refusal of life's prospects. Significantly, Pool's architecture shines in the phenomenal world, not an alleged hereafter. For heroic spirits, assurance in the one assuages uncertainty of the other. As Joseph Campbell explains, to witness "not the world of solid things but a world of radiance" requires a "visionary transformation" of the mundane,[47] faith in the beauty of the "here and now" (*SS*, 417). With comic persistence, "The Emerald" casts its light into the shadows of disbelief.

Once again, Barthelme invokes myth as the source of moral enrichment. Contrary to the uncompromising seriousness of Judeo-Christian religion, notes Campbell, myth tolerates an irreverent union of humor and symbolism as it performs its revelations (220). It is a fitting choice for an ethical ironist. In "The Emerald," Barthelme reveals the gods' presence in the most unlikely vessels: the witch Mad Moll and a reliquary encasing the Foot of Mary Magdalene. Sharing the same initials, the two form a sisterhood of darkness and light, a coalition as ambiguous as the emerald's portent. But as Moll ultimately concludes, one cannot forego the heroic "scrabble for existence" (*SS*, 417) to worry whether life's mysteries are good, bad, or indifferent.

Conceived on a stormy night, Moll bears suspicious stigmas: a black beard and a furry black mark on her forehead. In a wild parallel to the Immaculate Conception, she claims to have endured a seven-year pregnancy to deliver a god's offspring, a sleeping, talking emerald, fathered by the man in the moon. In the midst of other provocative numerical configurations, the child's arrival "at six sixty-six in the evening" (*SS*, 394) further darkens the omens. Though an acceptable tale in antiquity, the story seems madness to her cynical contemporaries. Yet Moll brews knowledge. In her "witch's head" swirl spells and incantations but also "memories of God," from whose sustaining hands she "fell . . . into the world" (*SS*, 410). Faced with a phalanx of doubt-ers, however, her magic and wisdom sometimes seem "*not enough*" (*SS*, 401).

Having abandoned the "tucked-away gods" (*SS*, 401), disbelievers constitute this story's greater populace. Like Dante's lost souls, they form a hierarchy of denial. Deferring to her husband's prejudices, Moll's mother drifts into doubt when she tries to disguise her daugh-ter's congenital oddities to make her look normal, common, anony-mous. Flatly dismissing Moll's tale, young ignorant Lily reduces the emerald's mystical conception to salacious details, such as the alleged father's "hideously engorged member" (*SS*, 392). Like those beyond the gates of Dis, the truly hopeless doubters are mercenary schemers. A pervert tries to peddle his own false idol in a dark alley. Lather, the editor of *World*, capitalizes on life's ugliness and terror. Thieves cal-culate the weighty stone's value in dollars per carat. Out of greed, bit-terness, or fear, they want to destroy this pretender to the gods. Their spirits, if not their purses, are bankrupt, as they petrify in their own iron-willed obstinancy.

Allied with the powerful Foot, loyal bodyguard Soapbox, the canine convert Tarbut, and her own green redeemer, Moll crusades for the spiritual enchantments still accessible to mortals. The gods, she tells Lily, "are not dormant or dead as has often been proclaimed by dummies" (*SS*, 416), but "to live twice" (*SS*, 404), as the ruthless Vandermaster demands, may indeed presume too much. Faith, action, love—these articulate spirit and consciousness in the deafening roar of the "ferocious Out" (*SS*, 399). Such human experience, says Joseph Campbell, elicits the "rapture of being alive" (5).

Overnight to Many Distant Cities

The physical, emotional, and intellectual sources of human rapture preoccupy much of the short fiction in *Overnight to Many Distant Cities*. A few pieces—"Conversations with Goethe," "Well we all had our Wil-lie & Wade records . . .," "Wrack," "Captain Blood"—softly hum the amusements or comforts of friendship. But human desire—sometimes random lust, more often sustained magnetism—seems in this collec-tion's stories the best hope for mortals to share anything akin to heroics or otherworldly bliss.

In "The Sea of Hesitation," for instance, narrator Tom routinely re-cords the detached pursuits of his self-indulgent acquaintances. Francesca obsesses about Robert E. Lee; Catherine, about Balzac. Jinka writes Tom hate mail. Their interests are frenetic, disconnected; Tom seems equally indifferent to each. Still, he repeatedly defends people's right to "do what they want to do" (*O*, 94). Any willful action, he suggests, is better than silence and immobility. Ironically, through most of the story, Tom himself seems incapable of decisive action. Recalling his work with "sensory deprivation studies" (*O*, 95), he admits that the inertia of hibernating in a cozy "black box" with "the white-noise generator standing in for the sirens of Ulysses (himself an early SD subject)" (*O*, 103) is a tempting alternative to bucking for a place in the world. However, his comparison to Ulysses, paradoxically "deprived" to prove he could *conquer* temptation and premature death, supports Tom's subsequent claim that such experimentation is not "will-lessness," but the pursuit of "Possibility" (*O*, 103). The degree of heroism is relative to one's world: in this "Age of Fear" (*O*, 99), any "behavior" seems to Tom "a small miracle" (*O*, 96).

As Ulysses bravely lurched over the treacherous deep, Tom now tugs along on his own low-grade odyssey. After reading several pages of this voyage's uneventful log, we must suspect, against Tom's and Moll's protests, that the gods are indeed "dormant or dead." Then, in the last vignette, life's best miracle befalls Tom: sudden passion for a woman at the newsstand. Love animates him with joy not glimpsed elsewhere in the story. Rapt with desire for this goddess, who wordlessly returns his ardor, "smash of glance on glance" (*O*, 103), his heroic "persona floats toward her persona, over the Sea of Hesitation" (*O*, 103), and he savors every detail of the mating ritual. This magnetism, however short-lived, reaffirms humanity's riches.

For gods and mankind alike, of course, love is not without folly. Forgetting his wife and propriety, another narrator abandons himself to glorious debauchery at the Hotel Terminus: "He has learned nothing from the gray in his hair; . . . he behaves as if *something* were possible, still" (*O*, 115). Lost to love "forever," he then suffers betrayal: "She comes toward him fresh from the bath, opens her robe. Goodbye, she says, goodbye" (*O*, 117). Unlike some of Barthelme's other tales of rejection, however, "Terminus" closes with no hint of regret. Likewise, the narrator of "The Sea" embraces love's immediate prospects, even though he knows that he will eventually discover "spiritual blemishes" (*O*, 104) in his mate. Desire inspires hope, if not discretion. This risky assent to possibility is the payoff for surviving the advancement of years. As the life-worn Henrietta philosophizes, "maturity" has blessed her with an appreciation for human prospects in "a rich world beyond the pale" (*O*, 87). One does not grow old, she assures her mate Alexandra, "while love is here" (*O*, 87).

Two of the bridge pieces in *Overnight* also boast the heroics of love. In "Now that I am older . . .," desire transforms ordinary food and furnishings into spiritual accoutrements. Noble sounding phrases— "fleet through the woods" (*O*, 132) instead of "came home from work," and "plucked forth a cobwebbed bottle" (*O*, 132) instead of "passed the Gallo"—likewise mask the vernacular. The speaker covets the ritual of flowers and feasts that anticipates the bed, but mostly he covets the bed. Like an "arrow from the bow" or "spear from the hand of Achilles" (*O*, 132) (he is in too much of a hurry to choose between these similes), he rushes to his lover, bearing posies and pop records in lieu of shield and sword. Contrary to "The Sea," this ardent meditation ignores life's dull parts. More significantly, it ignores death. Above the bed where the lovers have enjoyed so many "violent nights" hangs a "silverprint" (*O*, 131) of violent death, its "prostrate forms" (*O*, 132) partially illumined by each morning's dawn. The speaker barely notes the gruesome omen before once again ravishing the lovely prone "form" beside him in "full light" (*O*, 132). The ironic analogy here between mortality's best and worst possibilities is unmistakable. For now, at least, life's coffers are full.

The other bridge piece—"I am, at the moment . . ."—is a strangely ethereal meditation, almost a hymn to death. Or maybe it is a hymn to memory, dream, imagination, the lighted altars of intellect. It is certainly a hymn to art. Like "They called for more structure . . ." and "A woman seated on a plain wooden chair . . .," the visionary text resonates with joy in the provocative beauty of words. The setting is a forest, but the cosmos that embraces this ethereal thicket is uncertain. Familiar earthly landmarks—Ireland, France, Portugal—are "remote" (*O*, 163) or "wrapped in an impenetrable haze" (*O*, 164), though the tombs amid the exotic "beanwoods" are "perfectly ordinary gray stone" (*O*, 163) and the "already-beautiful" wear crowns of "red kidney beans" (*O*, 164). Typically, Barthelme's woods are lively places, where old gray wolves romp after nymphs. "Departures," for instance, depicts the narrator's grandfather gamely bartering with the dryad Megwind, who is "lovely as light" (*F*, 102). But the forest of "I am, at the moment . . ." is hushed, holy, lighted by someone beloved who religiously glues "chandeliers" (*O*, 163) to the beanwood limbs. All Barthelme's woods, however, harbor mystery, and often miracles. As the narrator of "Departures" confesses, he is only "fantasizing" (*F*, 102) the forest and its denizens, but imagination's sorcery can conjure extraordinary visions to lighten the load of "human affairs" (*O*, 165).

Several images in "I am, at the moment . . ." suggest that this dreamy vision is another analog to death, not the physical wreckage of the last piece's silverprint, but the soul's contemplated release. Sometimes the speaker seems formless, otherworldly, physically remote from his lover. He sleeps in the tombs with the "already-beautiful," who, like Demeter's devotees, dance mystical rites. There are also redemptive overtones. After confession, "thieves" lie with the "deans of the chief cathedrals" (*O*, 164) in the woods. And the speaker confides, "This life is better than any I have lived, previously" (*O*, 164). Though he "rise[s] . . . to hold the ladder" (*O*, 163) for his beloved and closely monitors her labors, moreover, the couple never explicitly communicates. In fact, he says that he has a testament of "notes, instructions, quarrels" (*O*, 163) that he has been intending to discuss with her but has not or cannot. Briefly frustrated, he imagines that passionately hitting his own brow might "fell [him] to the earth" (*O*, 163). Some images, on the other hand, tauntingly imply that this vision is just another sexual fantasy, more well disguised than most. The "already-beautiful," who tote around "plump red hams" (*O*, 163), dance with "bronze hares," which the speaker has cast at night with much hot, sweaty, rhythmic labor: "Working the bellows, the sweat, the glare. The heat. The glare" (*O*, 164). Dancing and coupling is again reminiscent of Demeter's rites. More clearly, in this enchanting life that the speaker so enjoys, "beautiful hips bloom and part" (*O*, 164). Thus, when the speaker excitedly follows this disclosure with news of his beloved's "sudden movement toward red kidney beans" (*O*, 164), the reader cannot be sure whether she is ascending his spiritual ladder or descending his torso.

"I am, at the moment . . ." creates the sort of dense, abstract lyrics that Barthelme knew might lose readers. Wisely, he placed it like a benedictory preface to the keystone of *Overnight to Many Distant Cities*, the story that shares the volume's title. All the demons of human relationships, in fact, are appeased in "Overnight," as maturity's tender mercies assuage the psychic losses of disappointment, familial conflict, aborted romances, and aging. If Barthelme mapped the previous piece's mazes and detours in exotic landscapes, he charts this story's settings in the everyday world, or at least in a tempered imagination's analogs to these locales. Paris, Stockholm, Taegu, and Berlin are distant only because memory displaces them to an ephemeral past. Tolerance and pleasure then balance the emotional investments in these sites.

The story condenses the journeys of a life into a fleeting chronicle, just as its spatial leaps circle the globe in a few pages. It is a deceptively spare microcosm. Italicized reminiscences announce each excursion. Some memories rankle a bit: in Paris, the speaker impatiently kicked his temperamental child; in Boston, he helped a divorcée load up her marriage spoils; in Taegu, too many swaggering generals demanded the spoils of rank. No matter how he watched his path, moreover, the narrator was always stepping into someone else's politics: swilling Stockholm's expensive J & B, he unwittingly supported the Swedish army; a "Warsaw Pact novelist" once inveigled him to smuggle "a package of paper" (*O*, 170) to the United States. Most pitiful, though, was the wretched loveless man in London, who gnawed his buttons for his soul's hunger. Selected for review along with these misfortunes, however, are ecstatic times shared with friends or lovers: a youthful escapade in Mexico City, more exciting to the elders who tracked the runaways than to the romantic adolescents themselves; simple "happiness" (*O*, 174) with a beautiful lover in Berlin; best of all, the celebration of Barcelona.

The Barcelona anecdote that closes the story departs noticeably from the context now expected of these recollections. To this point, the narrator has substantiated his memories almost exclusively with "real" objects and places. The people, though sometimes exaggerated, are likewise credible. Contrarily, the Barcelona anecdote resumes the dreamy tone and sublime images of "I am, at the moment. . . ." Again, the persona seems both quick and dead. At first, the italics hint no mystery: "*In Barcelona the lights went out*" (*O*, 174). Probably just an electrical short; hence, the candlelit dinner of "shiny langoustines" (*O*, 174). Later, strolling with his lover, the narrator celebrates the repeatedly blissful state of marriage: "Show me a man who has not married a hundred times," he boasts, "and I'll show you a wretch who does not deserve the world" (*O*, 174). Through the anecdote's first paragraph, then, nothing more than mortal romance seems to inspire his rapture for Barcelona. Yet in the next paragraph, he is suddenly and quite mysteriously dining with "the Holy Ghost" (*O*, 174) and discussing Barcelona's lighting difficulties. The passage ends just as ambiguously: "In an ecstasy of admiration for what is we ate our simple soup" (*O*, 174).

Here, again, is the now familiar apotheosis of life as is, with faith edging out irony in death's final play-off. Is Barthelme structuring another analog between a freely creative intellect and a blissful, otherworldly spirit? Very possibly. An infinite cosmos, "Overnight" suggests, exists in memory, dream, and imagination. But the god of this cosmos is just an ordinary mortal, listening to Manhattan's forecast— "tomorrow, fair and warmer, warmer and fair, most fair. . . ." (*O*, 174)—as he eats his "simple soup." All in all, it is a good life, Barthelme wrote. Bless the bean waters of Babel.

The Legacy: Tickets to Paradise

By the late 1980s, people were accustomed to Barthelme's shameless irreverence for short story form: his absences, his arias, his fiction's chameleon poses. But acceptance had its laggards. For instance, colleague Raymond Carver, once suspicious of Barthelme's motives, tried to make peace by honoring "Basil from Her Garden" in *Best American Short Stories, 1986*. When Barthelme subsequently dissected this particular fiction and scattered it through *Paradise*, Carver felt betrayed. Had he known "Basil" was to be part of a novel, he grumbled, he would not have considered it. Carver's chagrin amused Barthelme. He wanted to redeem good will, to tell Carver that, at the time, he himself did not know the story's destiny. Neither, of course, could Barthelme have imagined his own life path when he wrote Damon Runyon parodies for his high school newspaper or hung shows in a Houston gallery or trailed his gods to New York City. In life, as in fiction, he trafficked in possibility.

Still, like most artists, most *people*, Barthelme succumbed to bouts of despair and abused his health. Seeing his thin books on the shelf next to other writers' thick books worried him. Sustaining a novel worried him. He used to say that his stories' tight, complex structures taxed intellect and patience; they were difficult to support in a sprawling network. The public's expectations fed this worry. Popular bias viewed short fiction as a stepchild unworthy of the novel's laurels. With his startling successes, however, Barthelme greatly altered this perception of short fiction and opened the genre for other generations to blaze their own trails into the "exquisite mysterious muck." As *Overnight to Many Distant Cities* indicates, moreover, maturity gave his work a patina of age, temperance, and grace. *Snow White* and *The Dead Father* were distant triumphs before he again successfully launched a novel, but even as Barthelme concentrated his last years' efforts on longer fiction, he never abandoned the rich veins mined in narrow spaces.

In March 1989 the *New Yorker* published its last short fiction from Barthelme before he died the following July. If not a dazzling performance, "Tickets" is one of those beautifully balanced meditations that returns pleasure with every reading.[48] Stylistically more conservative than the lyric abstractions in *Overnight*, it confirms the even hand of the settled writer. Because Barthelme's stature in American short fiction owes so much to the longevity of his relationship with this magazine, "Tickets" deserves a cameo shot.

Barthelme once said that his favorite sentence was not a sleek liner, but an old "wreck," curious for all its odd baggage.[49] Without straining to the limits of "Sentence" or "Bone Bubbles," "Tickets" assembles a whole fleet of these fastidiously constructed wrecks—true treasures in Barthelme's legacy. The narrator's role in the fiction's dilemma supports these semantic freighters perfectly. From the first postured sentence, the narrator tries to muster the impression that he is inured to social politics. His wife has tickets to the symphony. Though she has politely invited the narrator to join "her group" (32)—her group consisting of herself and her thick, thick friend Morton—she knows full well that her husband does not like to suffer the discomforts of sitting all evening. Meanwhile, the artist Barbet has invited the narrator's wife and Morton to join *his* group. Fueled by the narrator's repressed jealousy, these simple gestures menace like rival nations' lying diplomacy. The sublimated emotion also generates the story's stylistic accretions. As staid subject-verb openings quickly collect clause upon clause, defense upon defense, obsessive thinking exposes the narrator's feigned control as mental paralysis. Suspended in his agitation, he cannot act—hence, the absence of plot.

Pleasure derives chiefly from comic exchanges within this tense design. The strongest stylistic pattern is an amusing "cancellation" motif. With "invitation" and "counter-invitation" (32), the narrator's wife and Barbet introduce this pattern in the story's first two paragraphs. In their game of social politics, each player checks the other's moves until he or she captures the opponent's men or women. After the narrator reviews his options for attending the symphony himself, the story compounds the game's significance. Dwelling on both Barbet's gall and his vicious "decayed wit" (33), the narrator explains midway through his mental volley that the artist's notoriety rests on his "'Cancellation' paintings" (33)—canvasses that superimpose an unknown work on a famous one and thereby invalidate the masterpiece. Like the terrorist writers Barthelme described in "After Joyce," Barbet manufactures objects hostile to both art and life. He betrays his creative gifts. Ironically, the narrator replicates this destructive process by defending Barbet's "fundamentally indefensible" (33) acts. With mock praise of the paint's value, for instance, he essentially cancels the importance of Barbet's art. However, he really wishes to cancel Barbet and suggests that the artist's "ill will" (33) justifies shooting the nuisance. The cancellation motif's real task, though, is to purge the jealous "ill will" that immobilizes the narrator in his obsessive thinking/counterthinking. Morton facilitates the resolution. Barbet hates Morton, but Morton counters Barbet's malice with an "indifference" that exacerbates the artist to "illness" (34). A riotous rug analogy, extended in one carbuncular sentence to almost 200 words, finishes off the malcontent. More importantly, Morton's role in Barbet's misfortune delights the narrator and thus cancels all "ill will" for his wife's friend. Checkmate.

This resolution returns the narrator to prospects declared in the story's opening sentence (forming his own group), but unbridled joy now vanquishes earlier restraint and inspires him to action. Rebelliously embracing Morton, a Gypsy, a blind man, and "that sugarplum" his wife, he proclaims that his new group "will exist in contradistinction to all existing groups" (34). His enthusiasm for life's wonderful charge will mobilize countless troops. Barthelme's trademark litany— here, "Let's go! Let's go!" sung "over and over" (34) with the signature faith of the later stories—spurs adherents into the mysterious welter.

Like a friendship of unexpected joy and duration, "Tickets" gives the kind of pleasure that makes good memories of good literature. Barthelme bequeathed many such gifts. Not the least was his legacy to his students, who remember him affectionately as a munificent magus with one gene from Legree. Though he never sent his style armies to trample other writers' sacred land, he did expect untested troops to bleed their native talents. According to former students Vikram Chandra (Sahaj) and Olive Hershey, reading one's feeble words aloud in class to the inexorable pacing of Barthelme's lizard cowboy boots could be murderous for a young writer unaccustomed to the master's scrutiny. Sometimes such a trial left the linoleum "littered with small carcasses."[50] No one, however, doubted Barthelme's motives for cutting his or her work to the quick. The master's radar, says Hershey, was "unerring": "As a teacher [Barthelme] gave the kind of criticism I could accept, e.g., 'Your sperm count is low,' 'Make her smarter,' or 'Try having her fall in love with the other guy.' He had an astounding gift as a listener, hearing work for the first time in class and knowing instantly where the story wanted/ needed to go."[51] In matchless acts of integrity, moreover, Barthelme generously donated his time, money, and energy to prepare his students to light their own ways. As much as his inimitable fiction, they will remember these gifts.

When Barthelme died, his literary estate included *Guilty Pleasures*, his "nonfiction" parodies/satires; *Sam's Bar: An American Landscape*, a picture-text collaboration with Seymour Chwast; *The Slightly Irregular Fire Engine*, his award-winning children's book; four novels (*The King*, published posthumously); and nine short fiction collections. Given their creative triumphs, all within three decades, these works constitute a staggering legacy. Translated into many languages, the short fictions alone extend Barthelme's importance to literature globally. These small fictions were the author's natural terrain. Here, on his existential journeys, Barthelme never dreamed utopian parks poised beyond an earthly pale. But he willed us something better: privileged glimpses of the world's gardens, lush with exquisite flaws. "Collect the troops!" his stories hail. "Let's go! Let's go!"

Notes to Part 1

1. See J. D. O'Hara, "Donald Barthelme: The Art of Fiction LXVI," *Paris Review* 80 (Summer 1981): 194–95; hereafter cited in the text.

2. Interview with author, 19 August 1988, in Houston, Texas; unless otherwise noted, all further background data and authorial comments are based on this interview.

3. See Jerome Klinkowitz, "Donald Barthelme," in *The New Fiction: Interviews with Innovative American Writers*, ed. Joe David Bellamy (Urbana: University of Illinois Press, 1974), 46–47; hereafter cited in the text.

4. *Donald Barthelme IV*, Pacifica Tape Library, BC2720.01–04, 1975.

5. Prefatory comment, *Guilty Pleasures* (New York: Farrar, Straus and Giroux, 1974); hereafter cited in the text as *GP*.

6. Raymond Federman, "Surfiction—Four Propositions in Form of an Introduction," in *Surfiction: Fiction Now . . . and Tomorrow*, ed. Raymond Federman (Chicago: Swallow Press, 1975), 8.

7. Robert Alter, *Partial Magic: The Novel as a Self-Conscious Genre* (Berkeley and Los Angeles: University of California Press, 1975), 25.

8. *Sixty Stories* (New York: G. P. Putnam's Sons, 1981), 97; hereafter cited in the text as *SS*.

9. See Jo Brans, "Embracing the World: An Interview with Donald Barthelme," *Southwest Review* 67 (Spring 1982): 127.

10. See Heide Ziegler, "Donald Barthelme," in *The Radical Imagination and the Liberal Tradition: Interviews with English and American Novelists*, ed. Heide Ziegler and Christopher Bigsby (London: Junction Books, 1982), 47; hereafter cited in the text.

11. "Not-Knowing," in *Voicelust*, ed. Allen Wier and Don Hendrie, Jr. (Lincoln: University of Nebraska Press, 1985), 45; hereafter cited in the text as *N*.

12. John Barth, "Title," *Lost in the Funhouse* (New York: Doubleday, 1968), 113.

13. *Come Back, Dr. Caligari* (Boston: Little, Brown, 1964), 4–5; hereafter cited in the text as *CB*.

14. *Snow White* (New York: Atheneum, 1967), 169; hereafter cited in the text as *SW*.

15. Wayne B. Stengel, *The Shape of Art in the Short Stories of Donald Barthelme* (Baton Rouge: Louisiana State University Press, 1985), 183; hereafter cited in the text.

16. Neil Schmitz, "Donald Barthelme and the Emergence of Modern Satire," *Minnesota Review* 1 (Fall 1971): 111.

17. An early example of Barthelme's interest in parodic caricature is *Amanda Feverish*, published in four weekly "chapters" under his pseudonym Bardley (University of Houston *Cougar*, October 1952). Subtitled a "deeply disturbing novel of the South," it is a ludicrous portrait of an intoxicated heroine with an unslakeable thirst for "Old Illusion."

18. Werner Spies, "The Laws of Chance," in *Homage to Max Ernst*, ed. G. di San Lazzaro (New York: Tudor Publishing Company, 1971), 17; hereafter cited in the text.

19. H. de Balzac, *Eugénie Grandet, the Country Parson and Other Stories*, trans. Ellen Marriage (Philadelphia: Gebbie Publishing Company, 1899), 1:125.

20. *Forty Stories* (New York: G. P. Putnam's Sons, 1987), 83; hereafter cited in the text as *F*.

21. William Stott, "Donald Barthelme and the Death of Fiction," *Prospects* 1 (1975): 369–86; hereafter cited in the text.

22. "After Joyce," *Location* 1 (Summer 1964): 15–16; hereafter cited in the text as *AJ*.

23. The narrator's plight is the sort of "instant Dada" a writer steals from daily life. It is apparently inspired by a conversation Barthelme overheard in a restaurant: "'But Henry, I've never *taught* in the daytime before.' *The Teacher From the Black Lagoon*" (quoted in O'Hara, 202).

24. By contrast, the poor god Hephaestus, denied mortals' "real goods," must settle for two golden mechanical women.

25. Donald Barthelme, William Gass, Grace Paley, and Walker Percy, "A Symposium on Fiction," *Shenandoah* 27 (Winter 1976): 24; hereafter cited in the text as *SF*.

26. Alan Spiegel, *Fiction and the Camera Eye: Visual Consciousness in Film and the Modern Novel* (Charlottesville: University Press of Virginia, 1976), 38; hereafter cited in the text.

27. Roland Barthes, *Critical Essays*, trans. Richard Howard (Evanston, Ill.: Northwestern University Press, 1972), 181; see Barthes's discussion of linguistic continuity in Butor's *Mobile*.

28. *Overnight to Many Distant Cities* (New York: G. P. Putnam's Sons, 1983), 9; hereafter cited in the text as *O*.

29. Jacques Ehrmann, "The Death of Literature," in Federman, *Surfiction: Fiction Now . . . and Tomorrow*, 245.

30. Raymond Federman, "Surfiction—Four Propositions," and Jean Ricardou, "Nouveau Roman, Tel Quel," suggest the terms "word-being" and "grammatical person," respectively, in their discussions of contemporary fiction's fragmented identities. See Federman's *Surfiction: Fiction Now . . . and Tomorrow*, 12–13, 112–19.

31. *Amateurs* (New York: Farrar, Straus and Giroux, 1976), 81; hereafter cited in the text as *A*.

32. *City Life* (New York: Farrar, Straus and Giroux, 1970), 117; hereafter cited in the text as *CL*.

33. Though he detested the word *ineffable*, Barthelme used it to suggest an elusive "knowledge" or "truth" that artists yearn to explore; see *SF*, 11.

34. The term *speaking pictures*, common in Elizabethan England, is adapted by Milton Klonsky, ed., in *Speaking Pictures: A Gallery of Pictorial Poetry from the Sixteenth Century to the Present* (New York: Harmony Books, 1975), especially 1–26; hereafter cited in the text.

35. *Donald Barthelme II*, Pacifica Tape Library, BC2720.01–04, 1975.

36. See J. H. Matthews, *The Imagery of Surrealism* (Syracuse, N.Y.: Syracuse University Press, 1977), 219.

37. John Leland, "Remarks Re-marked: Barthelme, What Curios of Signs!" *Boundary 2*, 5 (Spring 1977): 797.

38. Morse Peckham, *Man's Rage for Chaos: Biology, Behavior, and the Arts* (New York: Schocken Books, 1967), 37; hereafter cited in the text.

39. "The Most Wonderful Trick," *New York Times Book Review*, 25 November 1984, 3.

40. Roland Barthes, "The Photographic Message," *Image-Music-Text*, trans. Stephen Heath (New York: Hill and Wang, 1977), 29.

41. Raymond Carver, "Barthelme the Scribbler," review of *Great Days*, in *Texas Monthly*, March 1979, 162.

42. Jerome Klinkowitz, *The Self-Apparent Word: Fiction as Language/Language as Fiction* (Carbondale: Southern Illinois University Press, 1984), 75.

43. "Basil from Her Garden," *New Yorker*, 21 October 1985, 36–39; hereafter cited in the text. Barthelme later dissected the dialogue and incorporated its parts into *Paradise*.

44. Towering Lyndon Baines Johnson, renowned for barbecue diplomacy at his Texas ranch, had inherited the presidency after John F. Kennedy's assassination and was campaigning for reelection when "The President" first appeared in the *New Yorker*, 5 September 1964.

45. Unlike "Basil from Her Garden," Barthelme left "A Manual for Sons" virtually intact for its role in *The Dead Father* after debut in the *New Yorker*. Appearing again in *Sixty Stories* cleansed of its most scurrilous impertinences, it remains one of the best examples of Barthelme's choral prose.

46. For a thorough discussion of Demeter's and daughter Persephone's roles in the death-rebirth rituals, see Robert Graves, *The Greek Myths*, 2 vols. (Baltimore: Penguin Books, 1960), 1:89–96; and Michael Grant, *Myths of the Greeks and Romans* (New York: New American Library, 1962), 126–38; hereafter cited in the text.

47. Joseph Campbell, *The Power of Myth*, ed. Betty Sue Flowers (New York: Doubleday, 1988), 230; hereafter cited in the text.

48. "Tickets," *New Yorker*, 6 March 1989, 32–34; hereafter cited in the text.

49. See Larry McCaffery, "An Interview with Donald Barthelme," in *Anything Can Happen: Interviews with Contemporary American Novelists*, ed. Tom LeClair and Larry McCaffery (Urbana: University of Illinois Press, 1983), 34.

50. Vikram Chandra [Sahaj], "Good-bye, Mr. B," *Texas Monthly*, July 1990, 48.

51. Olive Hershey, letter to author, 19 May 1989.

Part 2

THE WRITER

Introduction

Among the finest gems in Barthelme's legacy are several substantial interviews and two essays rich with insights into three decades' writing. Typically, Barthelme crafted all these—even the seemingly spontaneous interviews—with the same worrying precision with which he tooled his short fiction. He did not like to spill his words recklessly into print. Ostensibly shy of microphones (he attributes a 1975 recorded interview/reading to a weak moment), he answered Jerome Klinkowitz's queries by mail. That early seventies' interview reveals personal, social, and professional influences frequently cited in later publications, but the parody of Joyce Carol Oates's criticism comically exposes the ironist's own hand. Likewise, though J. D. O'Hara's interview evolved from a weekend's congenial musings and philosophical flights, Barthelme polished the transcript to its final elegance. To accompany excerpts from these and Larry McCaffery's dialogues, he similarly chose and edited remarks from our 1988 discussion. In their entirety, these interviews boast not only wise statements of intent on which to hang Barthelme's stories, but also curious anecdotes about painters, musicians, other writers, his family, odd amusements, and private grievances.

Until the publication of "Not-Knowing" (1983), however, Barthelme's critics based their analyses chiefly on statements in "After Joyce" (1964), the earlier of two invaluable essays framing the author's visions. In that seminal work, Barthelme contended that contemporary art is not a mirror of life, but an autonomous object, as contrary as the world it inhabits. Trying to shake loose its riddles is a purposeful exercise for wending through life's mazes. In the following excerpt from "Not-Knowing," he reassesses that lofty claim even as he defends art's essential mystery.

Taken together, these selected comments illuminate the humor, political pique, and artistic passion that inspired so much of Barthelme's work.

Interview with Jerome Klinkowitz

Jerome Klinkowitz: When you improvise, do you think of the chord changes or the melody?

Donald Barthelme: Both. This is an interesting question which I'm unable to answer adequately. If the melody is the skeleton of the particular object, then the chord changes are its wardrobe, its changes of clothes. I tend to pay rather more attention to the latter than to the former. All I want is just a trace of skeleton—three bones from which the rest may be reasoned out. . . .

Klinkowitz: In Richard Schickel's *New York Times Magazine* piece last year, you were reported as saying that "The principle of collage is the central principle of all art in the twentieth century in all media." Would you care to expand and perhaps tell me how it specifically applies to fiction?

Barthelme: I was probably wrong, or too general. I point out however that New York City is or can be regarded as a collage, as opposed to, say, a tribal village in which all of the huts (or yurts, or whatever) are the same hut, duplicated. The point of collage is that unlike things are stuck together to make, in the best case, a new reality. This new reality, in the best case, may be or imply a comment on the other reality from which it came, and may be also much else. It's an *itself*, if it's successful: Harold Rosenberg's "anxious object," which does not know whether it's a work of art or a pile of junk. (Maybe I should have said that anxiety is the central principal of all art in the etc., etc.?). . . .

Klinkowitz: In your story "See the Moon" one of the characters has the line, "Fragments are the only forms I trust." This has been quoted as a statement of your aesthetic. Is it?

Barthelme: No. It's a statement by the character about what he

Excerpted from "Donald Barthelme," in *The New Fiction: Interviews with Innovative American Writers*, ed. Joe David Bellamy (Urbana: University of Illinois Press, 1974), 45–54. © 1974 by the Board of Trustees of the University of Illinois. Reprinted by permission of the University of Illinois Press.

is feeling at that particular moment. I hope that whatever I think about aesthetics would be a shade more complicated than that. Because that particular line has been richly misunderstood so often (most recently by my colleague J. C. Oates in the *Times*) I have thought of making a public recantation. I can see the story in, say, *Women's Wear Daily:*

WRITER CONFESSES
THAT HE NO LONGER
TRUSTS FRAGMENTS

TRUST "MISPLACED,"
AUTHOR DECLARES

DISCUSSED DECISION
WITH DAUGHTER, SIX

WILL SEEK "WHOLES"
IN FUTURE, HE SAYS

CLOSING TIME IN
GARDENS OF WEST
WILL BE EXTENDED,
SCRIVENER STATES

New York, June 24 (A&P)—Donald Barthelme, 41-year-old writer and well-known fragmatist, said today that he no longer trusted fragments. He added that although he had once been "very fond" of fragments, he had found them to be "finally untrustworthy."

The author, looking tense and drawn after what was described as "considerable thought," made his dramatic late-night announcement at a Sixth Avenue laundromat press conference, from which the press was excluded.

Sources close to the soap machine said, however, that the agonizing reappraisal, which took place before their eyes, required only four minutes.

"Fragments fall apart a lot," Barthelme said. Use of antelope blood as a bonding agent had not proved. . . .

Interview with Larry McCaffery

Larry McCaffery: At the end of your story "Sentence," your narrator says that the sentence is "a structure to be treasured for its weaknesses, as opposed to the strength of stones." Am I right in assuming that one of the things that interests you the most about the sentence as an object is precisely its "treasured weaknesses"?

Donald Barthelme: I look for a particular kind of sentence, perhaps more often the awkward than the beautiful. A back-broke sentence is interesting. Any sentence that begins with the phrase, "It is not clear that . . ." is clearly clumsy but preparing itself for greatness of a kind. A way of backing into a story—of getting past the reader's hardwon armor.

McCaffery: Can you describe what's happening once you've found this initial impulse? Obviously you aren't aiming at developing characters or furthering the plot or whatever else it would be that most writers would say.

Barthelme: A process of accretion. Barnacles growing on a wreck or a rock. I'd rather have a wreck than a ship that sails. Things attach themselves to wrecks. Strange fish find your wreck or rock to be a good feeding ground; after a while you've got a situation with possibilities. . . .

McCaffery: Your narrator in "See the Moon?" comments enviously at one point about the "fantastic metaphysical advantage" possessed by painters. What was he referring to?

Barthelme: The physicality of the medium—there's a physicality of color, of an object present before the spectator, which painters don't have to project by means of words. I can peel the label off that bottle of beer you're drinking and glue it to the canvas and it's there.

Excerpted from "An Interview with Donald Barthelme," in *Anything Can Happen: Interviews with Contemporary American Novelists*, ed. Tom LeClair and Larry McCaffery (Urbana: University of Illinois Press, 1983), 32–44. © 1983 by the Board of Trustees of the University of Illinois. Reprinted by permission of the University of Illinois Press.

McCaffery: Like a lot of painters in this century, you seem to enjoy lifting things out of the world, in this case words or phrases, and then . . .

Barthelme: And then, sung to and Simonized, they're thrown into the mesh.

McCaffery: But what you're doing—this rearrangement of these "real" elements into your own personal constructions—is related to collage, seems to partake of some of that metaphysical advantage you're describing.

Barthelme: This sort of thing is of course what Dos Passos did in the Newsreels, what Joyce did in various ways. I suppose the theater has the possibility of doing this in the most immediate way. I'm on the stage and I suddenly climb down into the pit and kick you in the knee. That's not like writing about kicking you in the knee, it's not like painting you being kicked in the knee, because you have a pain in the knee. This sounds a bit aggressive. Forgive me.

McCaffery: Another aspect of painting that seems relevant to your fiction is the surrealist practice of juxtaposing two elements for certain kinds of effects—in fiction or poetry, different sorts of language.

Barthelme: It's a principle of construction. This can be terribly easy—can become cheapo surrealism, mechanically linking contradictions. Take Duchamp's phrase, in reference to *The Bride and the Bachelors*, that the Bride "warmly refuses" her suitors. The phrase is very nice, but you can see how it could become a formula.

McCaffery: How do you avoid falling into this trap in your own work? Is there a formula for avoiding the formula?

Barthelme: I think you stare at the sentence for a long time. The better elements are retained and the worse fall out of the manuscript. . . .

McCaffery: At the end of the title story of *City Life*, Ramona comments about "life's invitations down many muddy roads": "I accepted. What was the alternative." I find a similar passivity in many of your characters—an inability to change their lot. Does this tendency spring from a personal sense of resignation about things, or are you trying to suggest something more fundamental about modern man's relationship to the world?

Barthelme: The quotation you mention possibly has more to do with the great world than with me. In writing about the two girls in

City Life who come to the city, I noticed that their choices—which seem to be infinite—are not so open ended. I don't think this spirit of "resignation," as you call it, has to do with any personal passivity; it's more a sociological observation. One attempts to write about the way contemporary life is lived by most people. In a more reportorial fiction one would, of necessity, seek out more "active" protagonists—the mode requires it, to make the book or story work. In a mixed mode, some reportage and some part play (which also makes its own observations), you might be relieved of this restriction. Contemporary life engenders, even enforces passivity, as with television. Have you ever tried to reason with a Convenience Card money machine? Asked for napkin rings in an Amtrak snack-bar car? Of course you don't. Still, the horizon of memory enters in. You attempt to register change, the color of this moment as opposed to the past or what you know of it.

McCaffery: Is it because you're dealing with this common kind of modern life that your characters so often seem concerned with coping with boredom?

Barthelme: I don't notice that so much. I think they're knitting lively lives—perhaps in subdued tones. Are you asking for T. E. Lawrence?

McCaffery: Hmmm. Maybe I should call this aspect of modern life "the cocoon of habituation that covers everything, if you let it," as your narrator in "Daumier" says.

Barthelme: Recently I've come to believe that, as one of the people in *Great Days* says, "Life becomes more and more exciting as there is less and less time." True, I think.

Interview with J. D. O'Hara

J. D. O'Hara: What starts your stories off?

Donald Barthelme: It's various. For instance, I've just done a piece about a Chinese emperor, the so-called First Emperor, Ch'in Shih Huang Ti. This came directly from my wife's research for a piece she was doing on medical politics in Chinatown—she had accumulated all sorts of material on Chinese culture, Chinese history, and I began picking through it, jackdaw-like. This was the emperor who surrounded his tomb with that vast army of almost full-scale terra cotta soldiers the Chinese discovered just a few years ago. The tomb, as far as I know, has yet to be fully excavated, but the scale of the discovery gives you some clear hints as to the size of the man's imagination, his ambition. As I learned more about him—"learned" in quotation marks, much of what I was reading was dubious history—I got a sense of the emperor hurrying from palace to palace, I gave him two hundred some-odd palaces, scampering, almost, tending to his projects, intrigues, machinations. He's horribly, horribly *pressed for time*, both actually and in the sense that many of his efforts are strategies against mortality. The tomb itself is a strategy, as is the imposition of design on the lives of his people, his specifications as to how wide hats shall be, how wide carriages shall be, and so forth.

"The Emperor" might be considered as another version of the story I did about Cortes and Montezuma, and both as footnotes to *The Dead Father*, another emperor.

O'Hara: You do your homework, in other words.

Barthelme: Everybody does, I think. Research yields things that you can react to, either accept or disagree with. My Montezuma and Cortes are both possibly nobler figures than responsible historians would allow, but I hope not implausible. There are conflicting versions

Excerpted from "The Art of Fiction LXVI," *Paris Review* 80 (Summer 1981): 181–210. © 1981 by the *Paris Review*. Reprinted by permission of the authors and the *Paris Review*.

as to how Montezuma died. I have him killed by a stone flying through the air, presumably from the hand of one of his subjects. The alternative is that the Spaniards killed him. I prefer to believe the former.

O'Hara: You take the Cortes-Montezuma friendship to have been a reality, not just a matter of political manipulation?

Barthelme: There seems to be little question that Cortes was a master manipulator. Still, he seems to have been genuinely impressed by Montezuma. Bernal, as you read his account of the Conquest, enlarges in a very respectful way on Montezuma's qualities, as priest-king at the center of an elaborate religious/political establishment, about which Cortes was wonderfully obtuse. It's as if you marched into present-day Salt Lake City at the head of your brave little group, listened politely and with interest to a concert by the Mormon Tabernacle Choir, sitting in the front row, and then whipped out your sword and claimed the state of Utah for Scientology.

O'Hara: Suppose a reader took the story's limousines and detectives to mean that you're being comic about it?

Barthelme: The limousines are only a way of making you see chariots or palanquins.

O'Hara: What about the woman's golden buttocks?

Barthelme: A way of allowing you to see buttocks. If I didn't have roaches big as ironing boards in the story I couldn't show Cortes and Montezuma holding hands, it would be merely sentimental. You look around for offsetting material, things that tell the reader that although X is happening, X is to be regarded in the light of Y. . . .

O'Hara: What about the moral responsibility of the artist? I take it that you are a responsible artist (as opposed, say, to X, Y, and Z), but all is irony, comic distortion, foreign voices, fragmentation. Where in all this evasion of the straightforward does responsibility display itself?

Barthelme: It's not the straightforward that's being evaded but the too-true. I might fix your eye firmly and announce "Thou shalt not mess around with thy neighbor's wife." You might then nod and say to yourself, quite so. We might then lunch at the local chili parlor and say scurrilous things about X, Y, and Z. But it will not have escaped your notice that my statement has hardly enlarged your cosmos, that I've been, in the largest sense, responsible to neither art, life, nor adultery.

I believe that my every sentence trembles with morality in that each attempts to engage the problematic rather than to present a proposition to which all reasonable men must agree. The engagement might be very small, a word modifying another word, the substitution of "mess around" for "covet," which undresses adultery a bit. I think the paraphrasable content in art is rather slight—"tiny," as de Kooning puts it. The *way* things are done is crucial, as the inflection of a voice is crucial. The change of emphasis from the what to the how seems to me to be the major impulse in art since Flaubert, and it's not merely formalism, it's not at all superficial, it's an attempt to reach truth, and a very rigorous one. You don't get, following this path, a moral universe set out in ten propositions, but we already have that. And the attempt is sufficiently skeptical about itself. In this century there's been much stress placed not upon what we know but on knowing that our methods are themselves questionable—our Song of Songs is the Uncertainty Principle.

Also, it's entirely possible to fail to understand or actively misunderstand what an artist is doing. I remember going through a very large Barnett Newman show years ago with Tom Hess and Harold Rosenberg, we used to go to shows after long lunches, those wicked lunches which are no more, and I walked through the show like a certifiable idiot, couldn't understand their enthusiasm. I admired the boldness, the color and so on but inwardly I was muttering "wallpaper, wallpaper, very fine wallpaper but wallpaper." I was wrong, didn't get the core of Newman's enterprise, what Tom called Newman's effort toward the sublime. Later I began to understand. One doesn't take in Proust or Canada on the basis of a single visit.

To return to your question: if I looked you straight in the eye and said, "The beauty of women makes of adultery a serious and painful duty," then we'd have the beginning of a useful statement.

O'Hara: Can you point out a specific too-true evaded in a specific story?

Barthelme: Perhaps in "The Death of Edward Lear." Charming into ferocious, Edward Lear into King Lear.

O'Hara: Wordsworth spoke of growing up "Fostered alike by beauty and by fear," and he put fearful experiences first; but he also said that his primary subject was "the mind of Man." Don't you write more about the mind than about the external world?

Barthelme: In a commonsense way, you write about the impingement of one upon the other—my subjectivity bumping into other subjectivities, or into the Prime Rate. You exist for me in my perception of you (and in some rough, Raggedy Andy way, for yourself, of course). That's what's curious when people say, of writers, this one's a realist, this one's a surrealist, this one's a super-realist, and so forth. In fact, everybody's a realist offering true accounts of the activity of mind. There are only realists.

Interview with Barbara Roe

Barbara Roe: What does this word *innovative* really mean, or does it mean anything in regard to fiction?

Donald Barthelme: I take it to be congratulatory, if imprecise. I doubt that there's much beyond new combinations of quite well-known maneuvers. "Make it new" as a battle cry seems naive today, a rather mechanical exhortation. If a piece of writing is of this time, of a particular time, that seems quite enough to ask of it.

Roe: But there's something exciting about the new. . . .

Barthelme: Very much so, there's a frisson there, but perhaps nothing lasting. I think it has to do with seeing something done well. Above all, we like to see something done well, and in writing, when it's done really well, there's always an element of freshness which is probably an aspect of craft but may appear to be an aspect of time, may appear to be "the new."

Roe: Or a response to new cultural or historical situations. . . .

Barthelme: That happens. These usually take a long while to understand or get an intuition about, but sometimes one has something to say immediately—as in response to a war one finds morally reprehensible. The Vietnam War shook up American writers, including those like myself too old to soldier. One suddenly finds oneself in a new relation to the government.

Roe: At Brown University last spring [1988], you, along with William Gass, John Hawkes, and Stanley Elkin, took part in a symposium on postmodernism organized by Robert Coover. What issues were discussed?

Barthelme: Some very tired ones, including "What is postmodernism?" The term is, after all, only one of a half-dozen equally unsatisfactory formulations, probably the one that has come closest to sticking. The chief misconception is that this kind of writing is meta-

Excerpted from an interview conducted in Houston, Texas, on 19 August 1988.

fiction, fiction about fiction. It's not. It is a way of dealing with reality, an attempt to think about aspects of reality that have not, perhaps, been treated of heretofore. I say it's realism, bearing in mind Harold Rosenberg's wicked remark that realism is one of the 57 varieties of decoration.

Roe: What about the term *experimental*, which is often applied to your work?

Barthelme: It's not quite a hostile remark, but it does contain within it the notion of the failed experiment. Something like "Bone Bubbles" was, yes, an experiment, and although I wouldn't suggest it was wholly successful, I thought it worth publishing. It's something I do along with a number of other things.

Roe: In his 1968 article "Dance of Death," John Aldridge criticized one of your collections for failing to dramatize the significant forces behind the everyday "dreck," for failing to reconcile the "apocalyptic" and the "doggy world."

Barthelme: The sentiment here is that I'm using dreck—playing with it, essentially—rather than condemning it in good rightminded fashion or analyzing the dynamics of its production in good leftminded fashion. I'd argue that I was probably doing something of both and that he didn't notice. Fiction is not academic argument.

Roe: During the 1960s, you defended the status of the art object *as object*, but in your recent "Not-Knowing," you seem to recant somewhat. What caused the change?

Barthelme: Both positions are defensible. The first idea, that the artwork is an object in the world in much the same way a dog bisquit or a mountain is an object in the world, is an effort to deny that the artwork is a rendering or a copy of the world. The second position attempts to be a little clearer about the relation between art and world, and I ended by saying that art is a meditation about the world rather than a reproduction of some aspect of the world. The two ideas are not directly contradictory. The relevant line is "Art is a true account of the activity of mind." I don't mean to suggest that that's all art is, merely that this is a place to begin. The statement does take into account the controversy about the truth value of art, does a bit of work there.

Roe: Do you expect readers to recognize the cohesive elements in your stories?

Barthelme: Feel rather than recognize. If the story is written well enough, there's enough built into it to make it cohere. Every reader will not get every reference, perhaps, or be hooked by every little hook. But if the thing is successful, there will be enough of that to bind the reader to the piece.

Roe: A few years ago, you seemed worried that perhaps a lack of emotion was a weakness in your stories.

Barthelme: A constant worry. I'm still worried. I tell my students that one of the things readers want, and deserve, is a certain amount of blood on the floor. I don't always produce it. Probably a function of being more interested in other parts of the process.

Roe: You use all sorts of language levels.

Barthelme: I mix levels, which is really not kosher but allows certain useful effects, like mixed media in painting. It's zone-crossing, sociologically speaking.

Roe: As a reader, I'm very aware that certain sentences or parts of sentences repeat, much as I notice a painting's repetitive line, form, or color.

Barthelme: Rhythm is important, and it's one of the things you notice about student work. Very often students don't, in the beginning, understand that their sentences are supposed to have certain rhythms and that the rhythms are part of the texture of the story. It's hard to teach, something that's more a knack than directly teachable. But it's central, it's a factor in every sentence, and you have to insist on it, remember to insist on it.

Roe: In "Not-Knowing," you said that art, ideally, should have a meliorative aspect, should change the world.

Barthelme: But I didn't say in what degree. The ambition, or necessity, if you will, is present, but the change might be very small. I like very much and have often quoted what de Kooning said about content in painting—"It's very tiny, content, something like a flash." This was in an interview with David Sylvester, I believe. And the degree to which any given piece of writing might be said to alter the world might also be tiny. But I don't want to lose sight of the impulse.

Roe: You've said that the problems of the contemporary writer arise from the contamination of language by all sorts of things—politics, commerce, philosophical cant. What are the problems of the ordinary American?

Barthelme: Americans have political problems which they don't recognize as political. The impoverishment of the country by the arms race is a good example. Money spent on arms is, among other things, useless money in terms of the economy because it's stored. It's in nerve gas, aircraft carriers, the Stealth bomber. I gave a reading at the University of Alabama a couple of years ago, and on the way to the campus, we passed an airfield packed with military aircraft, trillions of dollars worth of planes stacked up there, National Guard stuff, not even first-line stuff. The cost, the weight of this, is not understood by most Americans. They don't know where their money's going. They know they're pressed for money and that their school systems are being eighty-sixed by national accrediting organizations, but they don't connect this to that National Guard elephant graveyard. Black people think they're poor because they're black and the white folks control the money. This is true, but black folks are damaged more by lousy economic policy than by racism.

Roe: You write about these social inequities?

Barthelme: I do. There is a consistent social concern in my stories from the 1960s to the present. Tends to be slipped in while your attention is directed toward something else. It's not Lincoln Steffens, and it's not Mike Harrington [twentieth-century American writers noted for scrutinizing social ills], but it's there. I'm not talking about the direct political satire in *Guilty Pleasures*, but rather an obligato, always present in everything—also, the worse the political situation, the more stimulating it is for the writer. Most of the pieces in *Guilty Pleasures* were written during the Nixon administration, when things were so egregiously wrong that we were on a continual ladder of amazement and outrage. The Reagan administration probably did as much damage to the country but in ways more difficult to identify. A great advantage Central European writers have is the absolutely miserable political conditions in their home countries. It's what gives Kundera his bite, his ability to be radical, go to the root. Outrages have been done him and his countrymen of a dimension we can barely intuit. He derives an insight into the dark side of human possibility from this, it informs his work every step of the way.

Roe: To what extent do you discuss writing with other writers or artists?

Barthelme: With someone like Grace Paley, who is a dear friend and who lives across the street from us in New York, there are always lots of things to talk about besides art because first we have the life of our street to worry about. Grace is very concerned with our street, and we have really significant conversations having to do with our street. For a long time we talked about the war because Grace was very much an antiwar activist. At a certain point she was arrested along with some colleagues for holding a protest on the White House lawn, a misdemeanor case, and we had to combat that and that took a lot of conversation. I did a *New York Times* op-ed piece about it in which I quoted Grace as saying that the protesters had walked on the lawn, wonderful line, "Very softly and carefully." And we had school conversations because both of us were teaching and PEN conversations and children conversations and some purely literary conversations. Grace does not have other than strong opinions except about lunch. She usually shows up at lunchtime and eats what is put before her with appropriate appreciative comment. So literature would be maybe 15 percent of the conversation. Grace is a Russian writer—Chekhov should do as well— we're different kinds of writers and that's interesting.

Roe: You and Raymond Carver seemed mutually appreciative of each other's work. He mentioned in *Alive and Writing* that you have had a tremendous impact on creative writing classes. You've been called one of the most imitated writers in America. Do you see this?

Barthelme: No, because I don't think the imitations, if they're there, get published. Carver would probably be the most imitated writer in America at the moment. I like his work and liked him, although I knew him very slightly.

Roe: Is the new generation of writers more concerned than their predecessors with politics, economics, and social class?

Barthelme: I think there are lowered expectations, not aesthetic expectations for the work, but lowered expectations in terms of life. My generation, perhaps foolishly, expected, even demanded, that life be wonderful and magical and then tried to make it so by writing in a rather complex way. It seems now quite an eccentric demand.

From "Not-Knowing"

Let us discuss the condition of my desk. It is messy, mildly messy. The messiness is both physical (coffee cups, cigarette ash) and spiritual (unpaid bills, unwritten novels). The emotional life of the man who sits at the desk is also messy. I am in love with a set of twins, Hilda and Heidi, and in a fit of enthusiasm I have joined the Bolivian army. The apartment in which the desk is located seems to have been sublet from Moonbeam McSwine. In the streets outside the apartment, melting snow has revealed a choice assortment of decaying et cetera. Furthermore, the social organization of the country is untidy; the world situation is in disarray. How do I render all this messiness, and if I succeed, what have I done?

In a commonplace way we agree that I attempt to find verbal equivalents for whatever it is I wish to render. The unpaid bills are easy enough, I need merely quote one: FINAL DISCONNECT NOTICE. Hilda and Heidi are somewhat more difficult. I can say that they are beautiful—why not?—and you will more or less agree, although the bald statement has hardly stirred your senses. I can describe them—Hilda has the map of Bolivia tattooed on her right cheek and Heidi habitually wears, on her left hand, a set of brass knucks wrought of solid silver— and they move a step closer. Best of all, perhaps, I can permit them to speak, for they speak much as we do.

"On Valentine's Day," says Hilda, "he sent me oysters, a dozen and a half."

"He sent me oysters too," says Heidi, "two dozen."

"Mine were long-stemmed oysters," says Hilda, "on a bed of the most wonderful spinach."

"Oh yes, spinach," says Heidi, "he sent me spinach too, miles and miles of spinach, wrote every bit of it himself."

To render "messy" adequately, that is, to the point that you are enabled to feel it—I don't want you to recognize only that it's there, it should, ideally, frighten your shoes—I would have to be more graphic than the decorum of the occasion allows. What should be emphasized is that one proceeds by way of particulars. If I know how a set of brass knuckles feels on Heidi's left hand it's because I bought one once, in a pawnshop, not to smash up someone's face but to exhibit on a pedestal in a museum show devoted to cultural artifacts of ambivalent status. The world enters the work as it enters our ordinary lives, not as a world-view or system but in sharp particularity: a tax notice from Madelaine, a snowball containing a résumé from Gaston.

The words with which I attempt to render "messy," like any other words, are not inert, rather they're furiously busy. We do not mistake the words *the taste of chocolate* for the taste of chocolate itself but neither do we miss the tease in *taste*, the shock in *chocolate*. Words have halos, patinas, overhangs, echoes. The word *halo*, for instance, may invoke St. Hilarius, of whom we've seen too little lately. The word *patina* brings back the fine pewtery shine on the saint's halo. The word *overhang* reminds us that we have, hanging over us, a dinner date with St. Hilarius, that crashing bore. The word *echo* restores to us Echo herself, poised like the White Rock girl on the overhang of a patina of a halo— infirm ground, we don't want the poor spirit to pitch into the pond where Narcissus blooms, eternally; they'll bump foreheads, or maybe other parts closer to the feet, a scandal—There's chocolate smeared all over Hilarius's halo, messy, messy. . . .

The combinatorial agility of words, the exponential generation of meaning once they're allowed to go to bed together, allows the writer to surprise himself, makes art possible, reveals how much of Being we haven't yet encountered. It could be argued that computers can do this sort of thing for us, with critic-computers monitoring their output; they're madly ambitious. When computers learn how to make jokes, artists will be in serious trouble. But artists will respond in such a way as to make art impossible for the computer. They will redefine art to take into account, that is, exclude, technology, photography's impact upon painting and painting's brilliant response being a clear and comparatively recent example.

The prior history of words is one of the aspects of language the world uses to smuggle itself into the work. If words can be contaminated by the world they can also carry with them into the work trace elements of world which can be used in a positive sense. We must allow ourselves the advantages of our disadvantages.

A late bulletin: Hilda and Heidi have had a baby, with which they're thoroughly displeased, it's got no credit cards and can't speak French, they'll send it back. . . . Messy.

Style is not much a matter of choice. One does not sit down to write and say: Is this poem going to be a Queen Anne poem, a Beidermeyer poem, a Vienna Secession poem or a Chinese Chippendale poem? Rather it is both a response to constraint and a seizing of opportunity. Very often a constraint is an opportunity. It would seem impossible to write *Don Quixote* once again, yet Borges has done so with great style, improving on the original, as he is not slow to tell us, while remaining faithful to it, faithful as a tick on a dog's belly. I don't mean that whim does not intrude; it does. Why do I avoid, as much as possible, using the semi-colon? Let me be plain: the semi-colon is ugly, ugly as a tick on a dog's belly. I pinch them out of my prose. The great German writer Arno Schmidt, punctuation-drunk, averages eleven to a page.

Style is of course *how*, and the degree to which *how* has become *what* since, say, Flaubert is a question that men of conscience wax wroth about, and should. If I say of my friend that on this issue his marbles are a little flat on one side, this does not mean that I do not love my friend. He, on the other hand, considers that I am ridden by strange imperatives, and that the little piece I gave to the world last week, while nice enough in its own way, would have been vastly better had not my deplorable aesthetics caused me to score it for banjulele, cross between a banjo and a uke. Bless Babel.

Let us suppose that I am the toughest banjulele player in town and that I have contracted to play "Melancholy Baby" for six hours before an audience that will include the four next-toughest banjulele players in town. We imagine the smoky basement club, the hustling waiters (themselves students of the jazz banjulele), Jacqueline, Jemima, Zeno, Alphonse, Gaston, Madelaine, Hilda and Heidi forming a congenial group at the bar. There is one thing of which you may be sure: I am not going to play "Melancholy Baby" as written. Rather I will play something that is parallel, in some sense, to "Melancholy Baby," based upon the chords of "Melancholy Baby," made out of "Melancholy Baby," having to do with "Melancholy Baby"—commentary, exegesis, elaboration, contradiction. The interest of my construction, if any, is to be located in the space between the new entity I have constructed and the "real" "Melancholy Baby," which remains in the mind as the horizon that bounds my efforts.

This is, I think, the relation of art to the world. I suggest that art is always a meditation upon external reality rather than a representation of external reality. If I perform even reasonably well, no one will accuse me of not providing a true, verifiable, note-for-note reproduction of "Melancholy Baby"—it will be recognized that this was not what I was after. Twenty years ago I was much more convinced of the autonomy of the literary object than I am now, and even wrote a rather persuasive defense of the proposition that I have just rejected, that the object is itself world. Beguiled by the rhetoric of the time—typified by a quite good magazine called *It Is*, published by the sculptor Phillip Pavia—I felt that the high ground had been claimed and wanted to place my scuffed cowboy boots right there. The proposition's still attractive. What's the right answer? Bless Babel.

A couple of years ago I visited Willem de Kooning's studio in East Hampton, and when the big doors are opened one can't help seeing— it's a shock—the relation between the rushing green world outside and the paintings. Precisely how de Kooning manages to distill nature into art is a mystery, but the explosive relation is there, I've seen it. Once when I was in Elaine de Kooning's studio on Broadway, at a time when the metal sculptor Herbert Ferber occupied the studio immediately above, there came through the floor a most horrible crashing and banging. "What in the world is that?" I asked, and Elaine said, "Oh, that's Herbert thinking."

Art is a true account of the activity of mind. Because consciousness, in Husserl's formulation, is always consciousness *of* something, art thinks ever of the world, cannot not think of the world, could not turn its back on the world even if it wished to. This does not mean that it's going to be honest as a mailman; it's more likely to appear as a drag queen. The problems I mentioned earlier, as well as others not taken up, enforce complexity. "We do not spend much time in front of a canvas whose intentions are plain," writes Cioran, "music of a specific character, unquestionable contours, exhausts our patience, the over-explicit poem seems . . . incomprehensible." Flannery O'Connor, an artist of the first rank, famously disliked anything that looked funny on the page, and her distaste has widely been taken as a tough-minded put-down of puerile experimentalism. But did she also dislike anything that looked funny on the wall? If so, a severe deprivation. Art cannot remain in one place, a certain amount of movement, up, down, across, even a gallop toward the past, is a necessary precondition.

Style enables us to speak, to imagine again. Beckett speaks of "the long sonata of the dead"—where on earth did the word *sonata* come from, imposing as it does an orderly, even exalted design upon the most disorderly, distressing phenomenon known to us? The fact is not challenged, but understood, momentarily, in a new way. It's our good fortune to be able to imagine alternative realities, other possibilities. We can quarrel with the world, constructively (no one alive has quarrelled with the world more extensively or splendidly than Beckett). "Belief in progress," says Baudelaire, "is a doctrine of idlers and Belgians." Perhaps. But if I have anything unorthodox to say, it's that I think art's project is fundamentally meliorative. The aim of meditating about the world is finally to change the world. It is this meliorative aspect of literature that provides its ethical dimension. We are all Upton Sinclairs, even that Hamlet, Stephane Mallarmé.

Part 3

THE CRITICS

Introduction

During the 1970s critics anxious to track new directions in literature acknowledged Barthelme as the forerunner of a maverick breed—Gass, Vonnegut, Coover, Kosinski—whose variously antic or defiant fictions resisted capture. According to Barthelme, a few pursuers bungled their own efforts. Attempting "to slap a saddle on this rough beast," they often missed a writer's intent.[1] Moreover, using such brands as parafiction, surfiction, or metafiction, critics focused almost exclusively on the renegade works as an art of surfaces, obsessed with the systems, signs, and symbols of its own making. For a few, though, resistance bred contempt; the latter denounced the new fiction's apparently unwarranted evasions. In "Not-Knowing," Barthelme briskly summarizes these errant attacks: "The criticisms run roughly as follows: that this kind of writing has turned its back on the world, is in some sense not about the world but about its own processes, that it is masturbatory, certainly chilly, that it excludes readers by design, speaks only to the already tenured, or that it does not speak at all, but instead, like Frost's Secret, sits in the center of a ring and Knows."[2] Ironically, Barthelme explains, this confusion of the "writer's task" arises from the world itself, from a contamination of language by the very culture that is the writer's subject or supposed field of reference. Exploited by television, advertising, and politics, language is now a wholesale commodity. Thus, the postmodernist has not abandoned his audience; rather, *he* has been deprived of readers. Theft, bludgeoning, and general skulduggery have impoverished his art.

To Barthelme's few detractors, however, this deprivation provides no justification for obscurity or paralysis. For instance, in "Dance of Death" (1968), a review of *Unspeakable Practices, Unnatural Acts*, John Aldridge counted Barthelme among Black Humorists and took the entire company to task for failing to help Americans recover from an "eclipse of imagination" or, worse, for deferring that charge to readers. While Aldridge praised a few stories for their creative power, he complained that too many immerse us in "dreck, the evacuated crud and muck of contemporary life," rather than dramatize the relationship be-

119

tween the "apocalyptic" and the "doggy life"—to his mind, the writer's chief mission.[3] Barthelme was similarly challenged by Joyce Carol Oates in "Whose Side Are You On?" (1972), where she railed against both his intellectual integrity and artistic design: "'Fragments are the only form I trust.' This from a writer of arguable genius, whose works reflect the anxiety he himself must feel, in book after book, that his brain is all fragments . . . just like everything else."[4] Then, midway through the seventies, Morris Dickstein, who had previously acclaimed the impassioned ingenuity of *City Life* (1970), lamented that, without sixties turmoil for inspiration, the stories in *Sadness* (1972) were just slick imitations, devoid of "vividness, emotion, actuality." Barthelme, he feared, had reached a "dangerous crossroads."[5]

The critical analyses that follow address complaints and prickly demands from all camps. As earlier indicated, Barthelme resolutely denied any zeal for "metafiction," or "fiction-about-fiction," perhaps because both its practice and its complementary critical perspective threaten to isolate art from life. Still, readers generally concede that pieces like "Bone Bubbles," "Sentence," and "The Glass Mountain" do scrutinize the process of their own creation. The first two analyses qualify, if not reconcile, this apparent contradiction. In the excerpt from *The Metafictional Muse* (1982), Larry McCaffery illustrates that surface vagaries—fragments, "dreck," discontinuous narration—are indeed poignant revelations of the contemporary world's malaise. From a similar perspective, Maurice Couturier and Régis Durand defend Barthelme's point that language contamination has short-circuited communication; neurotic speeches spring from egos (or deposed superegos) chronically displaced by American culture's shifting ground. Contrary to Aldridge's complaint, however, these verbal displacements do not necessarily cast readers "adrift in a sea of orbiting psychic garbage" (Aldridge, 90). Regardless of characters' angst, the awkward utterances of dialogue or narration are typically humorous and thus abate the otherwise dismal effects of "la vie quotidienne." Moreover, Couturier and Durand explain, since humor depends upon comic displacements and the complicity of its constituents, artist, text, world, and reader remain "intimately connected."

The last two selections—excerpts from Lee Upton's "Failed Artists in Donald Barthelme's *Sixty Stories*" (1985) and Alan Wilde's *Middle Grounds* (1987)—best parry Morris Dickstein's concern that Barthelme's stories must replace metafictional stasis with "vividness, emotion, actuality." Lee Upton proposes that the psychic defeats of Barthelme's artists are both cathartic and meliorative. Idling among the ruins of a fallen world, these surrogates offer haunting, albeit ephemeral, glimpses of higher orders, "greater possibilities." Alan Wilde's more ambitious analysis defends how Barthelme's fiction repeatedly braces mankind with possibility in his quest to resurrect values. The best of Barthelme's art, he asserts, is really *midfiction;* suspended between the extremes of metafiction and realism, the extraordinary fabric of these narratives generates mystery, even as it encourages us "to perceive, obliquely and ironically, the moral perplexities"[6] of an ordinary, temporal existence. Of the four critics, only Wilde explicitly supports the insistence by Barthelme that his "every sentence trembles with morality" (*O'Hara*, 199).

Writers William H. Gass and and Raymond Carver provide an interesting afterword (perhaps even *moral*) to this history of critical rivalries. In a 1968 review of *Unspeakable Practices, Unnatural Acts*, Gass chastised Barthelme for sometimes compromising art with "cleverness"; notably, he dismissed "Robert Kennedy Saved from Drowning" as "simply cheap."[7] Raymond Carver's review of *Great Days* echoed Gass's reservations.[8] But by the mid-1980s both colleagues had forgiven or better understood Barthelme's seeming transgressions. In a blurb printed with "Paradise before the Egg" (1986), for instance, Gass celebrates Barthelme's gifts to short fiction: his wit, his poetry, his magic.[9] Similarly, Raymond Carver later admits that until he read *Sixty Stories*, he had not appreciated Barthelme's inspiring virtuosity: "Barthelme has done a *world* of work, he's a true innovator who's not being devious or stupid or mean spirited or experimenting for experimenting's sake. He's uneven, but then who isn't?"[10] The moral, if there is one, is this: In earlier unsettled times, angry or suspicious critics may have misunderstood or overlooked artistic gifts that later critics assessing two or three decades' work more readily discover and value. Thus, as Mad Moll tells Lily, "the world may congratulate itself that desire can still be raised in the dulled hearts of the citizens by the rumor of an emerald."[11] It is fair for Carver to suggest that Barthelme's efforts sometimes falter. In the best stories, however, golden buttocks, halos, and emeralds obtain. Actuality is never enough.

Notes

1. See J. D. O'Hara, "Donald Barthelme: The Art of Fiction LXVI," *Paris Review* 80 (Summer 1981): 209; hereafter cited in the text.

2. Donald Barthelme, "Not-Knowing," in *Voicelust*, ed. Allen Wier and Don Hendrie, Jr. (Lincoln: University of Nebraska Press, 1985), 41.

3. John W. Aldridge, "Dance of Death," *Atlantic Monthly*, July 1968, 89–91; hereafter cited in the text.

4. Joyce Carol Oates, "Whose Side Are You On?" *New York Times Book Review*, 4 June 1972, 63.

5. Morris Dickstein, "Fiction Hot and Kool: Dilemmas of the Experimental Writer," *TriQuarterly* 33 (Spring 1975): 269–72.

6. Alan Wilde, *Middle Grounds: Studies in Contemporary American Fiction* (Philadelphia: University of Pennsylvania Press, 1987), 34.

7. William H. Gass, "The Leading Edge of the Trash Phenomenon," review of *Unspeakable Practices, Unnatural Acts*, by Donald Barthelme, *New York Review of Books*, 25 April 1968, 5–6.

8. Raymond Carver, review of *Great Days*, by Donald Barthelme, *Texas Monthly*, March 1979, 162–63.

9. Gass's apotheosis appears in *Esquire*, August 1986, 46.

10. See *Alive and Writing*, ed. Larry McCaffery and Sinda Gregory (Urbana: University of Illinois Press, 1987), 77.

11. Donald Barthelme, "The Emerald," *Sixty Stories* (New York: G. P. Putnam's Sons, 1981), 416.

Larry McCaffery

The title of one of Barthelme's best short stories, "Critique de la Vie Quotidienne," offers a good summary of what has always been the principal focus of his fiction: the attractions and frustrations offered by ordinary modern life. As Alan Wilde suggests in his perceptive examination of Barthelme's work, it is this scaled-down range of interests which may be what is most distinctive about his work: "The articulation [is] not of the larger, more dramatic emotions to which modernist fiction is keyed but of an extraordinary range of minor, banal dissatisfactions . . . not anomie or accidie or dread but a muted series of irritations, frustrations, and bafflements."[1] Certainly the reaction of Barthelme's characters to "la vie quotidienne" is easy to summarize, as a few of their remarks pointedly indicate:[2]

Excerpted from *The Metafictional Muse: The Works of Robert Coover, Donald Barthelme, and William H. Gass*, by Larry McCaffery (Pittsburgh: University of Pittsburgh Press, 1982), 101–5. © 1982 by University of Pittsburgh Press. Reprinted by permission of the University of Pittsburgh Press. A few minor inaccuracies have been silently corrected.

I was happier before.

Like Pascal said: "The natural misfortune of our mortal and feeble condition is so wretched that when we consider it closely, nothing can console us."

I've been sorry all my life!

I spoke to Sylvia. "Do you think this is a good life?" The table held apples, books, long-playing records. She looked up. "No."

The paradigmatic artistic experience is that of failure. . . . The world *is* unsatisfactory; only a fool would deny it.

Nearly all of Barthelme's work to date has been permeated by this overwhelming sense that life is not as good as we expected it to be—"The world in the evening seems fraught with the absence of promise," says the disgruntled narrator of "La Critique." This lack of satisfaction on the part of Barthelme's characters is produced by a series of closely connected personal anxieties which are neatly balanced by Barthelme's own evident artistic anxieties and the anxieties presumably experienced by Barthelme's readers. Indeed, there is a significant relationship in Barthelme's fiction between his *characters'* struggles to stay alive, to make sense of their lives, and to establish meaningful connections with others, and *Barthelme's* own struggle with the disintegration of fictional forms and the deterioration of language. Often Barthelme's self-conscious, metafictional approach allows these struggles to operate concurrently within the stories (many of his main characters even being surrogate artist figures), the two serving to reinforce or symbolize each other. Meanwhile, we *ourselves* provide a third aspect of this relationship: as we grapple with the elements to organize and make sense of them, we provide an additional sort of analogue or reflection of this struggle with disintegration. The relationship between these personal and metafictional concerns can be seen more clearly in the following schematic listing:

PERSONAL	METAFICTIONAL
Ennui with life's familiarities (both animate and inanimate); ongoing personal fight against the "cocoon of habituation which covers everything, if you let it" (*S*, p. 179)	Anticipation of the reader's sense of boredom; need to invent new revitalized literary forms

Sense of personal, political, and social fragmentation	Impulse toward collage, verbal fragmentation, free association, and other methods of juxtaposition to break down familiar sense of order
Inability to sustain relationships with others (especially women)	Inability to rely on literary conventions (linear plots, notions of cause and effect, realistic character development, etc.) which tie things together into a pleasing whole
Sexual frustration and anxiety; sense of impotence and powerlessness in comparison with others	Artistic frustration and anxiety; belief that art is useless and can never effect significant change
Inability to know; impulse to certainty blocked (and mocked) by lies, disguises, simplistic formulas, and the irreducible mystery of life	Refusal to explain or clarify, denial of hidden or "deep meanings" with tendency instead to "stay on the surface"
Inability to communicate with others; frustrating sense that language blocks or betrays the feelings one wishes to express	Suspicion that language has become "dreck," so full of "stuffing" and clichés that meaningful communication with an audience is impossible
Inability to create change in one's condition, a condition made more difficult by one's self-consciousness which serves to paralyze one from spontaneous, possibly liberating, activities	Sense that one must accept language's limits and its trashy condition (hence the "recycling tendency," with clichés and dreck being transformed into new objects); self-consciousness making the telling of traditional stories impossible

In Barthelme's fiction, then, the sources of dissatisfaction as well as the means of coping with it are intimately connected for both the artist and the ordinary person. Although the specific manifestations are varied, these parallel struggles often have to do with the attempt to maintain a fresh, vital relationship with either words or women—an obsession which is evident in the works of many other contemporary male metafictionists such as Gass, Coover, Barth, Sukenick, and Federman. Moreover, Barthelme's characters are typically shown not only to be painfully aware of their own personal and sexual inadequacies but, more generally, to be disgruntled or bored with the systems they rely on to deal with their fragmented, meaningless lives. Simply stated, their fundamental problem is twofold: on the one hand, they are bored with their humdrum lives and humdrum relationships with others and are therefore constantly seeking a means of overcoming their rigidly patterned but ultimately inconsequential lives; on the other hand, Barthelme's characters fear any loss of security and are unable fully to open themselves to experience because they find it so confusing, ambiguous, and unstable and because they don't trust the systems at their disposal for coping with it. Paradoxically, then, their very awareness of the dismal realities around them makes it all the more difficult for them to face up to the frightening moment when they must go forth and confront "the new." The narrator of "Subpoena," after being forced to dismantle his "monster-friend" Charles, offers a good summary of these mixed feelings: "Without Charles, without his example, his exemplary quietude, I run the risk of acting, the risk of risk. I must participate, I must leave the house and walk about" (*S*, p. 116). Even more pointed are the remarks of the narrator of "The Dolt" (possibly Barthelme himself) regarding a would-be writer's inability to think of anything to say: "I myself have these problems. Endings are elusive, middles are nowhere to be found, but worst of all is to begin, to begin, to begin" (*UP*, p. 65).

Thus, the question for Barthelme's characters remains: given a reality which is chaotic, and given the fact that the system of signs developed by man to help him deal with reality is inadequate—"Signs are signs, and . . . some of them are lies," says the narrator of "Me and Miss Mandible"—how does one generate enough humanly significant, exciting moments to insure that one is alive? Certainly one cannot rely on any exterior systems to help find assurances and solutions. As Alan Wilde suggests, "In a general way, what Barthelme takes his stand against are pretentions to certainty and the insistence on perfection; large demands and great expectations; dogmatisms and theories of all kinds."[3] Like Coover's characters, then, Barthelme's characters find themselves constantly confronting worn-out systems which fail to operate successfully—systems such as the government, the church, the military, the news media, and a changing series of intellectual systems. (Psychiatry, existentialism, literary criticism, and Freudian psychology are among Barthelme's favorite targets.) Indeed, Barthelme often seems to suggest, perhaps playfully, that the acceptance of any final claims to truth and certainty may result in a deadening of our ability to respond naturally to experience. In "The Photographs," Barthelme suggests precisely this point when he has one scientist suggest to another that they should burn the photographs they have discovered of the human soul:

> "It seems to me to boil down to this: Are we better off *with* souls, or just possibly *without* them?"
> "Yes. I see what you mean. You prefer the uncertainty."
> "Exactly. It's more creative. Take for example my, ah, arrangement with your wife, Dorothea. Stippled with uncertainty. At moments, we are absolutely *quaking* with nonspecific anxiety. *I* enjoy it. *Dorothea* enjoys it. The humdrum is defeated. Momentarily, of course."
>
> *(GP,* pp. 158–59)

As Barthelme well knows, any solution to casting off this "cocoon of habituation"—which deadens our responses to art, to other human beings, and to ordinary reality—can only be provisional in nature. But the key for Barthelme, just as it was for Coover, lies in our "keeping the circuits open," in our remaining open to experience sufficiently so that new responses and new systems can be produced to generate the freshness and vitality we all seek.

Notes

1. Alan Wilde, "Barthelme Unfair to Kierkegaard: Some Thoughts on Modern and Postmodern Irony, *Boundary 2,* 5 (Fall 1976): 51.
2. The following passages are taken from Donald Barthelme, *City Life* (New York: Farrar, Straus & Giroux, 1970), 78; *Come Back, Dr. Caligari* (Boston: Little, Brown, 1964), 177; *Sadness* (New York: Farrar, Straus & Giroux, 1972), 9, 93, 95; *Unspeakable Practices, Unnatural Acts* (New York: Bantam, 1969), 3; henceforth these works will be abbreviated as *CL, CB, S,* and *UP.* Also cited will be *Guilty Pleasures* (New York: Farrar, Straus & Giroux, 1974), abbreviated as *GP.*
3. Wilde, "Barthelme Unfair to Kierkegaard," 56.

Maurice Couturier and Régis Durand

In Barthelme's stories, there is almost always "a playful disruption of our accepted forms of discourse and understanding."[1] But his concern is not merely (not even perhaps primarily) with *forms;* rather it is with the interaction between the real (its signs and its meaning) and the self (its imaginative power and its emotions). Form is the result of this interface, language the best index to it, the very locus of the tensions, the disorder, the entropy that result. Barthelme's references to language as waste, *dreck,* to the "trash phenomenon," are well known. Often, as in *Snow White,* his strategy is to turn the condition to an advantage, to make a comedy of it with a kind of "camp" aesthetic enjoyment:

> We like books that have a lot of *dreck* in them, matter which presents itself as not wholly relevant (or indeed, at all relevant) but which, carefully attended to, can supply a kind of "sense" of what is going on. This "sense" is not to be obtained by reading between the lines (for there is nothing there, in those white spaces) but by reading the lines themselves—looking at them and so arriving at a feeling not of satisfaction exactly, that is too much to expect, but of having read them, of having "completed" them. (*SW,* p. 106)

Clichés, tags, scraps of everyday conversations, old quotes, are reassuring because of their low degree of activity, because of their inertia. But, whenever you speak, there is a danger that something will start vibrating frantically, will slip off your tongue, run amok: "'There are worms in words!' the general cries. 'The worms in words are, like Mexican jumping beans, agitated by the warmth of the mouth.'" ("A Pic-

Excerpted from *Donald Barthelme,* by Maurice Couturier and Régis Durand (New York and London: Methuen, 1982), 26–29. © 1982 by Maurice Couturier and Régis Durand. Reprinted by permission of Methuen and Co. Quoted passages may be found in *Snow White* (Bantam, 1968), *Unspeakable Practices, Unnatural Acts* (Farrar, Straus and Giroux, 1968), and *City Life* (Farrar, Straus and Giroux, 1970); some punctuation and page numbers have been silently changed to reflect these standard editions.

ture History of the War," *UPUA*, p. 142). This proneness to Brownian agitation is inherent in the act of speech itself. And the fear of the frantic disorder and disruption that may ensue is the reason why enunciation sometimes turns into an extraordinary adventure, a painful and hazardous extraction:

> I wanted to say a certain thing to a certain man, a certain true thing that had crept into my head. I opened my head, at the place provided, and proceeded to pronounce the true thing that lay languishing there—that is, proceeded to propel that trueness, that felicitous trularity, from its place inside my head out into world life. The certain man stood waiting to receive it. His face reflected an eager acceptingness. Everything was right. I propelled, using my mind, my mouth, all my muscles. I propelled. I propelled and propelled. I felt that trularity inside my head moving slowly through the passage provided (stained like the caves of Lascaux with garlic, antihistamines, Berlioz, a history, a history) toward its début on the world's stage . . . ("A Picture History of the War," *UPUA*, pp. 135–36)

This wonderful piece of linguistic comedy has affinities with the Woody Allen type of burlesque fantasy; at the same time it is not unrelated, from a psychological point of view, to the discourse of obsessive neurotics. Speech is difficult, but there are reasons for the difficulty, the ambivalent retention/excretion of the speaker. Once delivered from its cavities, its festering recesses, speech proliferates. It takes over, subverts—and the subversion causes anxiety and depression: "What is 'wailing'? What is 'funky'? Why does language subvert me, subvert my seniority, my medals, my oldness, whenever it gets a chance? What does language have against me—me that has been good to it, respecting its little peculiarities and nicilosities, for sixty years?" (*UPUA*, pp. 139–40). Once free, language is tentacular, predatory; it ensnares and dissolves. Every utterance is an aggression, a cannibalistic dispossession: "The moment I inject discourse from my u. of d. [universe of discourse] into your u. of d., the yourness of yours is diluted" (*SW*, p. 46). Hence the reassuring quality of *dreck*. Hence also the satisfaction in the minimal achievement outlined above: to have reached the end of a line, of a sentence, to have "completed" them. Portrait of the artist as antisemiotician, as post-Beckettian minimalist.

You can counteract the threat of proliferation and loss of sense by clutching at little things, the flotsam and jetsam of language. But you can also, in a classical reversal, desire (or act as if you desired) the loss itself, even though it is the negation of all coherent discourse. In Swift's Academy of Lagado, the concepts (the "signified") are lacking—which makes it necessary to turn to the things themselves (the "referent") in order to communicate: you carry your whole vocabulary on your back. In Barthelme's "Paraguay," in order to face the stress of proliferation, you can buy ingredients to mix with language, to thin it, with a pinch of silence—or a pinch of noise (that which does not make sense): "In the larger stores silence (damping materials) is sold in paper sacks like cement. Similarly, the softening of language usually lamented as a falling off from former practice is in fact a clear response to the proliferation of surfaces and stimuli. Imprecise sentences lessen the strain of close tolerances. Silence is also available in the form of white noise" ("Paraguay," *CL*, p. 24). Barthelme is telling us here in effect that displacement is the nature of language, not only synchronically and superficially (along the surfaces and encounters of everyday life), but also in depth, diachronically.

Every language is historical: it does not become poorer or disintegrate; it only changes with the culture. Barthelme's language is intimately bound up with contemporary American culture, and with the crises and changes that shape it. The language he writes in (and about) is a displaced idiom, an idiom of displacement. And, as with all displaced bodies, empty spaces, scars and longings are perceptible, even though there may be an attempt to conceal them behind a playful acceptance or justification (and perhaps even desire) of what is essentially unacceptable, unjustifiable—the loss of all values and points of reference. Caught in a double bind, Barthelme's language (and through him the language of the culture) is a deeply neurotic one, from which only some fragments will emerge, having escaped entropy, noise or sheer drivel: the celebrated "fragments," of course, but also lists, repertories and catalogues: "'The only form of discourse of which I approve,' Miss R. said in her dry, tense voice, 'is the litany'" ("The Indian Uprising," *UPUA*, p. 8).

This "theory" of language is cultural, but it is also psychological. It goes inevitably with a certain perception not only of the connections between culture and individual speech, but also of the connections between an individual and his or her own language. Barthelme's fiction, as we shall see, stages a central speaking voice or subject, with a weak sense of identity, constantly seeking refuge in fantasy, word-play or self-pity, endlessly playing games of delusion which barely conceal a terror of failure, loss and disintegration. The two aspects implied in the concept of displacement (topological as well as psychological) are perfectly in evidence here, and they come together in one essential element of Barthelme's fiction: *humour.*

Note

1. John Leland, "Remarks Re-Marked: Barthelme, What Curios of Signs!" *Boundary 2,* 5 (Spring 1977), pp. 795–811. But Leland's working theory of fragmentation—"To fragment presupposes some whole in the first place capable of being fragmented, just as the fragment, incomplete in itself, presupposes a whole or totality which 'completes' it" (p. 795)—is limiting, in precisely the way outlined and criticized by [Maurice] Blanchot. For another example of a superficial view on fragmentation, see J. Hendin in D. Hoffman (ed.), *The Harvard Guide to Contemporary American Writing* (Cambridge, Mass.: Belknap Press of the Harvard University Press, 1979): "Fragmentation of character and narrative often serve as devices for allaying anxiety" (p. 241).

Lee Upton

Failure seems to be one certainty in Donald Barthelme's *Sixty Stories.* His artists inevitably fail, within their work, to meet the full implications of their visions; failure becomes the good artist's lot. Some of Barthelme's artists may be simply poor artists, doomed to repetition, their art, we suspect, no more vital than the mass produced marketplace forms they abhor. Some of Barthelme's artists' values, like those of Hilda and Maggie in "Conservatory" and "Farewell," may be falsely dependent on the hallmarks of commercial success and exclusivity rather than on the actual process of creating art. These artists, furthermore, may be doomed to fail before those who depend on them and anxiously await some token of success. (Women, especially, make stern witnesses to failure in Barthelme's fiction.) More often than not, these artists are financially broke.

Excerpted from "Failed Artists in Donald Barthelme's *Sixty Stories,*" *Critique* 26 (Fall 1984): 11–17. © 1984 by the Helen Dwight Reid Educational Foundation. Reprinted by permission of the Helen Dwight Reid Educational Foundation. Published by Heldref Publications, 4000 Albermarle St., N.W., Washington, D.C. 20016.

But what may be especially interesting about these artist's failures is a species of haunting that occurs. These artists, poor or not-so-poor, may be haunted by the phantoms of art forms from the past, forms that appear to be outmoded in a contemporary vision that is more contingent, more rich, I think, in ambiguous insinuations. And as readers we may find these artists failing in songs, stories, and sculptures because their work is curiously dependent on absences. We are haunted as readers by our own intuition of what might be there—a fuller encounter with human emotions, less deflation and evasion. When these characters are most inarticulate, we may feel we know them best. A sort of complicity between reader and creation is evoked. Perhaps we are all players in life's minor leagues, haunted by intuitions of a higher order, haunted by the knowledge that there might be better songs to sing. Yet at points when Barthelme limns the terrain of failure, movements toward higher registers of emotion seem to flare. In a contemporary life where gestures toward certainty and transcendence may no longer be trusted, such gestures return briefly within some of these stories. While these artists fail to break through their limitations, moments arise that enclose the grand gesture in a way that is simultaneously comic, telling, and somehow powerful—as if "a *tremendous* peep" is, at times, in order.

Barthelme's letter-writer in "The Sandman" addresses failure directly: "Let me point out, if it has escaped your notice, that what an artist does is fail. . . . The actualization fails to meet, equal, the intuition. There is something 'out there' that cannot be brought 'here.' This is standard. I don't mean bad artists, I mean good artists. There is no such thing as a 'successful artist' (except, of course, in worldly terms)."[1] It is the impossibility of realizing our own intuitions that Barthelme asserts in his short stories. Readers must be aware of the artists' failure to create works with full resonance in such stories as "The Abduction from the Seraglio," "How I Write My Songs," "The Falling Dog," and "The Dolt." In turn, a tribute to the sublime, to possibility, briefly arises in such stories as "A Shower of Gold," "The Death of Edward Lear," and "The Phantom of the Opera's Friend." An impulse toward the grand gesture is presented, but such an impulse is inevitably preceded by emphasis on the comic and degrading limitations that overwhelm the character.

"The Abduction from the Seraglio" provides one possible starting point from which to discuss stories in which the reader is made aware of the artist's failure. A sculptor, the narrator makes giant foods; in

131

turn, his world view is titanic, ludicrously inflated. He creates 4,000 pound artichokes while at the same time he envisions a wealthy Plymouth dealer in romanticized terms as a Pasha. Constanze, the artist's former lover, is viewed as seized and held within the Plymouth dealer's Butler building which, in turn, the artist dramatizes as a seraglio. Reality, like the artist's structures, is titanic, a highly ordered gigantism. Even the story's title is an inflation; there is no seraglio and there is certainly no abduction. It is as if the sculptor, for all his exuberance, envisions his life in the borrowed terms of 1940s matinees, replete with faces made enormous on the screen and the compulsory imperiled woman.

Like some of Barthelme's other artists, the sculptor creates identical forms. While he is critical of businessmen as undifferentiated "rat poison salesmen" who are "rollin rollin rollin" on the asphalt vistas, he too is singing one song, creating repetitive forms in his art and even in his plaintive lyrics to Constanze. Yet, as an artist, the sculptor thinks in terms of his art continually. His language derives from his tactile sense, his manner of handling his materials. His comment that *War and Peace* is "terrible thick" (371) is not only comic for its accent on a misplaced quality, it also underscores his world view; as a sculptor he sees the world in terms of physical form, size. Now in a creative lapse, he composes songs to Constanze that reproduce themselves, are repetitive as his art forms or the screen of inflation and romance that he will place upon experience:

> Oh Constanze oh Constanze
> What you doin' in that se-rag-li-o?
> I been sleepin' on paper towels
> Sleepin' on paper towels and
> Drinkin' Sea & Ski
> Ever since I let you go.
>
> (370)

These lyrics convey his isolation in a mixture of pathos and comedy, yet fail to attempt the higher registers of emotional suggestion. Curiously, they are hymns to deflation, lack of possibility. We are made keenly aware of what is not there—the absence not only of Constanze, but of lyrics that suggest the full implications of loss.

Likewise, the lyrics of the songwriter in "How I Write My Songs" point up the failure of possibility. Narrated by a songwriter who might, for all we know, be part of a correspondence school course advertised on a matchbook cover, the story concerns a songwriter who is successful by commercial standards. He has "gone gold." Yet his songs fail to be more than comic repetitions, inane and unworthy of the inflated claims the songwriter makes for himself, those claims which rise in a delightfully soft-headed voice at the story's conclusion: "I will continue to write my songs, for the nation as a whole and for the world" (423). Like the narrator who emerges in the concluding lines of "The Dolt," this songwriter too finds it hard to begin creating; his solution is to take his openings from those of other songwriters. The songs he writes, like those in "The Abduction from the Seraglio," are inane and comic in a pathetic and yet telling way:

> When I lost my baby
> I almost lost my mine
> When I lost my baby
> I almost lost my mine
> When I found my baby
> The sun began to shine.
>
> (420)

These are what sell—daft lyrics about losing. The tone of these instructions on song-writing, a strange mixture of humility, braggadocio, and earnestness, is comic as well. Within these lyrics is a malaise, a blend of understated hilarity, cliché, and deflation: "Show'd my soul to the woman at the 7-Eleven / She said: Is that all?" (421).

A similar tone evolves in "The Falling Dog." The sculptor's immediate reaction to the dog that falls upon him is to set up cause—a vignette in which he is degraded by a beautiful woman seeking only to use his services. As the sculptor catalogues his reactions to the dog, he shifts through possibilities. Both the Falling Dog and the Yawning Man, the sculptor's previous form, reflect the mass-produced emphasis of the sculptor's society. Both images are of domesticity and automatic response—a dog once set falling cannot very well stop himself, just as a man who begins yawning may have a difficult time stifling his yawn. The artist's final reaction involves no judgment of significance. He feverishly lifts the dog, now destined to supplant the outmoded and exhausted (on every level) image of the Yawning Man. Just as the narrator of "The Abduction from the Seraglio" creates multiple images, a tendency that identifies him with the Plymouth dealer he despises and envies (who also deals in identical forms), so too the narrator of "The Falling Dog" settles upon one image that he will repeat obsessively. At the same time, despite the sculptor's vitality and playfulness, we are given no cue to lead us to believe that meaning will be discovered through the image of the dog or even that such an image will be fully experienced beyond variations upon clichés dealing with dogs. The sculptor's shifts through possibilities seem more mechanical than inspired. . . .

Yet Barthelme will also offer among his failed artists gestures that invoke a romantic sublime. In "A Shower of Gold," Peterson, an out-of-luck sculptor, appears on the program *Who Am I?* The television show specializes in humiliating its guests who must, in order to be eligible to appear, relate their problems in psychological terms rather than with the simple language that will not, finally, anesthetize or generalize loss. After nightmarish sequences in which Peterson's responsibilities mount, he appears on *Who Am I?* hoping to earn money. In his final lines, Peterson's words rise in sharp contrast to the tone of comic degradation that preceded them: "'My mother was a royal virgin,' Peterson said, 'and my father a shower of gold. My childhood was pastoral and energetic and rich in experiences which developed my character. As a young man I was noble in reason, infinite in faculty, in form express and admirable, and in apprehension . . .' Peterson went on and on and although he was, in a sense, lying, in a sense he was not" (23).

This "yes and no" Barthelme ending suggests that, although Peterson is not Perseus and therefore no god's son, in some ways Peterson and the rest of us must retain our own grand gestures. Peterson's final cry is a rallying away from the life-restricting humiliations he has witnessed, whether couched in psychoanalytical terms or the slick superficiality of television programs that invade and cheapen private lives. Peterson's status as human being—with all the limitations we may now see among ourselves—still allows him to, for one moment, create a fiction of himself that evades the television analysts' life-restricting and deadening conceptualizations. He has turned confession on its head. Rather than reciting degrading tales of an unfulfilled life, tales that would make *Who Am I?* ratings soar, Peterson reminds us that, schmucks as we may be, we may also, in some sense, be children of the gods. Peterson's grand gesture can survive in the face of the limitations that have been vividly presented throughout the story. It is as if, in Barthelme, the high claim, the upper registers of emotions, the fictions that deal with the gods and man's claim to be worthy of both salvation and sin, can be evoked if the narrative has been drenched with enough anxiety and fear sequences that deflate. A call to the gods would be false if not placed in the context of the contemporary diminishments that men and women face. As Tony Tanner suggests, "It is this combination of play and dread which makes [Barthelme's] odd personal fantasies seem so appropriate to contemporary America."[2] It is this ambiguous mix of emotions which affects us.

The same forces, in part, are at work in "The Death of Edward Lear." For his death, Lear, "nonsense writer and landscape painter," is surrounded by guests. Lear will wear "an old velvet smoking jacket and his familiar silver spectacles with tiny oval lenses" (365), the stereotypical uniform of the gentleman author of an earlier age. Lear will offer bedside wisdom on cats and children. His last action—that most significant moment in conventional narratives—will be to pick up "an old fashioned pen" (367). Such a death bed action points to the death of an old artistic order, the author, as cliché has it, ready to parley words on any subject including cats and children with certainty. While we can view Lear's death as the demise of an old order of a certain type of fiction that had seemed more sure-footed, less contingent, what most animates the story, saving it from dwindling into a simple sketch, are its last lines. The guests of Edward Lear will regularly perform his death scene and Lear will be transformed: "The supporting company plays in the traditional way, but Lear himself appears shouting, shaking, vibrant with rage" (367). The doddering, foolish old man of a gentler order emerges as Shakespeare's Lear, a fool, perhaps, but of another sort altogether, suggesting the high tragic scale that men and women can achieve; for all our limitations, the extraordinary can still surface.

Of all the stories that offer a moment of tragic dimensions, "The Phantom of the Opera's Friend" seems most explicit. The Phantom too is a failed artist, a musician, the possessor of "an immense buried talent" (139). He would be brought back into society by a modern friend who anxiously wishes to aid the Phantom and yet at times guiltily longs for a more normal, less tragic allegiance. The Phantom would live on a scale based on the concepts of an earlier time. His music is muffled by the concrete of the temporary; his romantic focus has lost meaning in the contemporary world: "His tentative, testing explorations in the city (always at night) have not persuaded him to one course or the other. Too, the city is no longer the city he knew as a young man. Its *meaning* has changed" [emphasis mine] (139). His home, deep within the opera house, has the plush and gorgeous furnishings of a nineteenth-century novel.

A plastic surgeon would metamorphose the Phantom, freeing him of the ugly scar tissue that finally distinguishes him. Like the psychoanalyst of "The Sandman," the surgeon would take dreams away; he would fit the Phantom of the Opera for a role in society less dramatic, surely trivialized. Despite his yearning for connection, the Phantom, not of his time, must remain in hiding. Yet such a Phantom, a creature of high art and high romance, continues to haunt contemporary life, as if our lives fail to meet our intuitions. Like the notes of an organ heard through several floors of concrete, the strains of new possibilities continue to haunt Barthelme's art, even while he and his readers may no longer retain confidence in high style and transcendency. In these stories Barthelme is, indeed, the Phantom of the Opera's friend, longing for a suitably less dramatic companion at times, yet paying homage, at least in a few brief notes, to an order of experience that assigned to men a place more sweeping, less attenuated. Loss is felt throughout such pieces; absence vivifies and makes pathetic, comic, and finally moving the words of these failed artists. The Phantom of the Opera's friend bemoans not only his own but our common lot: "I sit down at the curb, outside the Opera. People passing look at me. I will wait here for a hundred years. Or until the hot meat of romance is cooled by the dull gravy of common sense once more" (143). The friction between romance and the limitations of common sense, between intuition and the limitations of our creative actions, enlivens Barthelme's art. "I do a lot of failing and that keeps me interested," Barthelme told Joe David Bellamy in an interview.[3] In Barthelme's art, failure is a working principle. To be haunted by a vision of greater possibilities, to fail to meet the demands of such a vision means, among other things, to have been blessed by the capacity of experiencing one's imagination fully. Jerome Klinkowitz writes that Barthelme's stories are "not conventional arguments in the dialectics of form, but imaginative volcanoes, radical stopgap measures to save experiences which might otherwise be eroded with our loss of traditional standards."[4] It seems to me that these stories are, in fact, "stopgap measures." In the artists' failures we may be made more aware, as readers, of those experiences Klinkowitz refers to: our dilemma in deciding how best to experience ourselves as humans. Yet in some of these stories the artists—those whom we most often think of as creative organizers—may briefly align themselves with full tragic dimensions, if not above the angels and certainly not exactly among the gods, at least in shaky step formation— almost, I think, happily—amid the *full* richness of an ambiguous and uncertain realm.

Notes

1. Donald Barthelme, *Sixty Stories* (New York: Dutton, 1982), 196. Subsequent references will be made within the text.
2. Tony Tanner, *City of Words: American Fiction: 1950–1970* (New York: Harper & Row, 1971), 401.
3. Donald Barthelme in *The New Fiction*, ed. Joe David Bellamy (Urbana: University of Illinois Press, 1974), 52.
4. Jerome Klinkowitz, *Literary Disruptions* (Urbana: University of Illinois Press, 1975), 77.

Alan Wilde

The best of Barthelme's stories and novels—"City Life," "Engineer-Private Paul Klee," "Rebecca," "The Death of Edward Lear," "The Great Hug," *The Dead Father,* and, not least, "The Emerald"—are in fact (to proceed further into heresy) *moral* studies of how to deal with a world it is impossible either to dismiss or to understand. The attempt in most of these to re-create value and meaning in the felt absence of either accounts for the oddly indeterminate status of these fictions, which are at once among the quirkiest and the most compelling in contemporary literature. Certainly, "The Emerald" gives full play to the odd and fantastic in the premise and development of its plot, which recounts the kidnapping of a precocious, talking, seven-thousand-and-

Excerpted from *Middle Grounds: Studies in Contemporary American Fiction*, by Alan Wilde (Philadelphia: University of Pennsylvania Press, 1987), 35–37. © 1987 by the University of Pennsylvania Press. Reprinted by permission of the University of Pennsylvania Press.

thirty-five-carat emerald, the offspring of Mad Moll (a rather limited and ineffective witch) and the man in the moon, and its subsequent recovery when a reliquary containing "the true Foot of Mary Magdalene"[1] kills Vandermaster, its abductor. And yet, however much the story's incidents lay stress on life's vagaries and absurdities, its techniques—the generally humdrum speech, the predominantly dialogic presentation, the consequent exclusion of comment by the narrator, and a cast of characters who largely assume the authenticity of the situation—all these make for a treatment that is, for the most part, deliberately and scrupulously ordinary. But to put the matter this way may be to suggest, unintentionally, the priority of the ordinary over the marvelous, whereas their relationship, as the evidence of style reveals, is one of mutual qualification. Barthelme's language is always, even when most seemingly matter-of-fact, slightly but persistently stylized, deviant, offbeat. Indeed, in its bland recycling of clichés, in its barely perceptible stiffening of the rhythms and patterns of colloquial prose, in its ubiquitous deployment of linguistic *chevilles* (all as if enclosing the discrete elements of discourse within invisible and ironic quotation marks), and in its not always recognized capacity for modulating on occasion, as in Moll's monologues, into a more ornate and rhetorical register—in all these ways, Barthelme's flexible style, the indelible signature of his midfictional status, serves as the concrete embodiment of a vision that recognizes life's overwhelming dailiness even as it celebrates the human potential for establishing within that dailiness small, unstable, and mysterious enclaves of significance and pleasure.

"The Emerald," to come back to it now, thematizes this double view as fully and suggestively as any of Barthelme's fictions; and in doing so it recapitulates and enlarges on the concerns of "Small Island Republics" and *The Making of Ashenden*. Thus Moll, with her "memories of God who held me up and sustained me until I fell from His hands" (p. 410), inhabits a fallen world. Her descriptions of it (along with the emerald's)—it is, variously, "this gray world of yours" (p. 398), "the ferocious Out" (p. 399), "the welter" (p. 411), and "the scrabble for existence" (p. 417)—indicate an attitude that is from first to last suspensive, accepting of its drab and fierce confusions. That attitude sets Moll and her child directly at odds with the other characters, for all of whom the emerald is the hypostatized object of a passionate quest for the extraordinary as something perfected, other, and apart: a variably interpretable means of correcting or overcoming life's insufficiencies. So "Lily the media person" (p. 404) and her "editor-king" (p. 407),

Mr. Lather (their newspaper, not coincidentally, is called *World*), are after the perfect story, the mob of weirdly-named but otherwise indistinguishable emerald-hunters after still more exotic, if more tangible, gain; but it is only Vandermaster, whose quest is the most outrageous and extreme, that need concern us here. Seeking nothing less than immortality—"In addition to my present life," he tells Moll, "I wish another, future life" (p. 404)—Vandermaster represents desire run wild. But not, perhaps, as wild as all that. The absoluteness of desire may be construed as, among other things, the recurrent dream of art's resolving grace, its power to achieve through form a stability beyond the reach of life's disorders. If this is so, Barthelme's story presents itself, along with Apple's and Elkin's, as a comment on modernism. That is, as "Small Island Republics" contests the idea that man is the measure and *Ashenden* the belief that primitivism offers a genuine alternative to aestheticism, so "The Emerald" gives the lie to the heterocosmic imagination and to the imperialism of art.

Here again, the comment—roughly, the valorization of postmodernism's preference for looser and less determined orders and for smaller, less perfect pleasures—is both structural and thematic; and what the antic choice and arrangement of events intimate, Mad Moll herself expresses. "Diamonds," she says, "are a little ordinary. Decent, yes. Quiet, yes. But *gray*." And she proceeds then, in paradoxical praise of various gems, all of which are by any usual reckoning more ordinary than the diamond, to assert, precisely, the extraordinariness of the ordinary: "Give me step-cut zircons, square-cut spodumenes, jasper, sardonyx. . . . But best of all, an emerald" (p. 416). The justification of the claim is the substance of Moll's central speech, in which she spells out for Lily's benefit the "meaning" of the emerald and in which, through her, Barthelme adds to his acceptance of the world his assent to its possibilities: "It means, one, that the gods are not yet done with us. . . . The gods are still trafficking with us and making interventions of this kind and that kind. . . . Two, the world may congratulate itself that desire can still be raised in the dulled hearts of the citizens by the rumor of an emerald. . . . Three, I do not know what this Stone portends . . . but you are in any case rescued from the sickliness of same" (pp. 416–17).

The "in any case" neatly qualifies the affirmation, as does the aposiopetic maneuver that leads Moll to suggest abruptly "a small offering in the hat on the hall table" (p. 417). Indeed, the swerve from the vatic to the mundane provides the note of ironic deflation, at any rate of reservation, one expects to find in Barthelme's work. On the other hand, one needn't take literally, as Moll does, the existence of those "tucked-away gods whom nobody speaks to anymore" (p. 401) to recognize on Barthelme's part the wish to restore, along with desire and diversity, some sense of mystery to a radically despiritualized world: the world to which, in other stories, his characters so often react with a kind of wry or aggrieved hopelessness. The phrase that best sums up this intention is perhaps Alejo Carpentier's *"lo real maravilloso"*: "the intrinsic quality of Latin-American experience," as Alastair Reid says, paraphrasing Carpentier and referring specifically to *One Hundred Years of Solitude*, "in which the wondrous and inexplicable are an essential part of ordinary perception."[2] The perception (central to American pop art and French surrealism, as well as to what we have come to call magic realism) is one that Barthelme shares, whether or not it surfaces in all of his fictions. "The Emerald" ends with one of his most felicitous expressions of it. "And what now? said the emerald. What now, beautiful mother?" To which comes the reply: "We resume the scrabble for existence, said Moll. We resume the scrabble for existence, in the sweet of the here and now" (p. 417).

Notes

1. Donald Barthelme, *Sixty Stories* (New York: G. P. Putnam's Sons, 1981), p. 395. The story originally appeared, with pictures and captions (Barthelme's?), in the November 1979 issue of *Esquire*, pp. 92–105.

2. Alastair Reid, "The Latin-American Lottery," *The New Yorker*, 26 January 1981, p. 109.

Chronology

1931   Born 7 April in Philadelphia, to Donald and Helen (Bechtold) Barthelme; oldest of five children (four boys, one girl)—all eventually writers of varying direction and note.

1933   Family begins residence in Houston.

1945–1948   Reporter for the *Eagle*, St. Thomas High School, Houston; 1946, honorable mention for *Scholastic Magazine* short story contest.

1948–1949   Associate editor, *Sequoyah 1948–49*, Lamar High School literary magazine; Poet Laureate of Texas Award for "Inertia"; fourth-place tie in *Scholastic Magazine* short story contest, for "Integrity Cycle"; fall, enters University of Houston to study journalism; intermittent enrollment through summer 1957 ends with "junior" standing.

1950–1952   Works in various editorial roles for the University of Houston *Cougar;* writes parodies, satirical pieces, and drama reviews for the *Cougar* (often as "Bardley"); and, beginning in 1951, critiques music, theater, and film for *Houston Post.*

1953   Drafted into the army and its newspaper staff to serve two years (Fort Polk, Japan, Korea).

1955   Resumes writing for *Post* until hired by University of Houston News Service.

1956   Successively becomes editor for two campus publications, *Acta Diurna*, the faculty newsletter, and *Forum*, a journal featuring work by leading art and literary figures.

1961   After serving two years in board and public relations roles for Houston's Contemporary Arts Museum, he leaves the University of Houston to become the museum's director; in *Contact*, publishes "The Darling Duckling at School" (retitled "Me and Miss Mandible" in *CB*) and launches his career in short fiction.

1962 Moves to New York City to edit *Location* for art world mentors Tom Hess and Harold Rosenberg.

1963 Publishes "L'Lapse," his first piece in the *New Yorker* (March 2); later collecting "L'Lapse" with other "nonfiction" in *GP*, Barthelme maintains that his first *story* to appear in the *New Yorker* is "The Piano Player" (31 August).

1964 Publishes *Come Back, Dr. Caligari*, first short fiction collection and an immediate critical success; essay "After Joyce" appears in first issue of *Location;* the journal folds after the second issue.

1965–1966 Receives Guggenheim Fellowship and lives in Denmark for a year; *CB* published in England, establishing his international audience.

1967 Publishes *Snow White*, a novel.

1968 Publishes *Unspeakable Practices, Unnatural Acts*, short fiction.

1970 Publishes *City Life*, including collage pieces and short fiction, to plaudits from *New York Times Book Review;* begins contributing unsigned "Comment" pieces to *New Yorker.*

1971 *Time* magazine lists *City Life* in its "Best Books of the Year"; publishes *The Slightly Irregular Fire Engine*.

1972 With John Barth's encouragement, takes his first teaching position at SUNY, Buffalo, replacing Barth as distinguished visiting professor; publishes *Sadness;* receives Morton Dauwen Zabel Award from the National Institute of Arts and Letters; *The Slightly Irregular Fire Engine* wins National Book Award for children's literature.

1973 Disclaims several forgeries appearing under his name in literary journals; publishes several *New Yorker* pieces under pen name "Lily McNeil"; teaches as visiting professor at Boston University.

1974 Publishes *Guilty Pleasures*, billed as "nonfiction"; begins teaching at CUNY.

1975 Publishes *The Dead Father*, a novel.

1976 Publishes *Amateurs*, short fiction; *Snow White* performed as "Rehearsed Reading" (program note) at American Place Theatre, New York City; receives Jesse H. Jones

Award from Texas Institute of Letters for *The Dead Father;* "Manfred" (contest story completed by Karen Shaw) appears in *New York Times Magazine.*

1978   Publishes *Here in the Village,* a collection of unsigned *New Yorker* columns.

1979   Publishes *Great Days,* short fiction.

1981   Publishes *Sixty Stories,* chronological selections chiefly from earlier books, to renewed critical and popular acclaim; begins teaching at University of Houston.

1982   *Sixty Stories* earns him nomination for National Book Critics Circle Award, PEN/Faulkner Award for Fiction, and *Los Angeles Times* Book Prize.

1983   Publishes *Overnight to Many Distant Cities,* short fiction, to widely mixed reviews; *Great Days,* a play based on short story by same title, performed at American Place Theatre, New York; delivers essay "Not-Knowing" at University of Alabama symposium.

1986   Publishes *Paradise,* a novel; program chair for 48th International PEN Congress in New York City.

1987   Publishes *Forty Stories,* chiefly selections from earlier books, and *Sam's Bar: An American Landscape,* a picture-text collaboration by mail and telephone with Seymour Chwast.

1988   Diagnosed with throat cancer; given favorable prognosis after both surgery and chemotherapy; participates with Fiedler, Hawkes, and Coover in Brown University conference on postmodernism; receives Prix de Rome.

1989   "Tickets," last story in *New Yorker,* appears 6 March; in June, returns ill from American Academy in Rome; dies of cancer, Houston, 23 July.

1990   *The King,* a novel, posthumously published.

Selected Bibliography

Primary Works

Collections

Amateurs. New York: Farrar, Straus and Giroux, 1976. Includes: "Our Work and Why We Do It," "The Wound," "110 West Sixty-first Street," "Some of Us Had Been Threatening Our Friend Colby," "The School," "The Great Hug," "I Bought a Little City," "The Agreement," "The Sergeant," "What to Do Next," "The Captured Woman," "And Then," "Porcupines at the University," "The Educational Experience," "The Discovery," "Rebecca," "The Reference," "The New Member," "You Are as Brave as Vincent van Gogh," "At the End of the Mechanical Age."

City Life. New York: Farrar, Straus and Giroux, 1970. Includes: "Views of My Father Weeping," "Paraguay," "The Falling Dog," "At the Tolstoy Museum," "The Policeman's Ball," "The Glass Mountain," "The Explanation," "Kierkegaard Unfair to Schlegel," "The Phantom of the Opera's Friend," "Sentence," "Bone Bubbles," "On Angels," "Brain Damage," "City Life."

Come Back, Dr. Caligari. Boston: Little, Brown, 1964. Includes: "Florence Green Is 81," "The Piano Player," "Hiding Man," "Will You Tell Me?", "For I'm the Boy Whose Only Joy Is Loving You," "The Big Broadcast of 1938," "The Viennese Opera Ball," "Me and Miss Mandible," "Marie, Marie, Hold On Tight," "Up, Aloft in the Air," "Margins," "The Joker's Greatest Triumph," "To London and Rome," "A Shower of Gold."

Forty Stories. New York: G. P. Putnam's Sons, 1987. Includes stories from previous collections and these new titles: "Chablis," "On the Deck," "Opening," "Sindbad," "Rif," "Jaws," "Bluebeard," "Construction," "January."

Great Days. New York: Farrar, Straus and Giroux, 1979. Includes: "The Crisis," "The Apology," "The New Music" [alteration of "Momma"], "Cortés and Montezuma," "The King of Jazz," "The Question Party," "Belief," "Tales of the Swedish Army," "The Abduction from the Seraglio," "The Death of Edward Lear," "Concerning the Bodyguard," "The Zombies," "Morning," "On the Steps of the Conservatory," "The Leap," "Great Days."

144

Guilty Pleasures ["nonfiction"]. New York: Farrar, Straus and Giroux, 1974. Includes: "Down the Line with the Annual," "Letters to the Editore," "That Cosmopolitan Girl," "Eugénie Grandet," "Snap Snap," "The Angry Young Man," "L'Lapse," "The Teachings of Don B.: A Yankee Way of Knowledge," "Swallowing," "The Young Visitirs [sic]," "The Palace," "The Dragon," "An Hesitation on the Bank of the Delaware," "The Royal Treatment," "Mr. Foolfarm's Journal," "Heliotrope," "And Now Let's Hear It for the Ed Sullivan Show!", "Bunny Image, Loss of: The Case of Bitsy S.," "The Expedition," "Games Are the Enemies of Beauty, Truth, and Sleep, Amanda Said," "A Nation of Wheels," "Two Hours to Curtain," "The Photographs," "Nothing: A Preliminary Account."

Here in the Village [nonfiction: unsigned *New Yorker* columns]. Northridge, Calif.: Lord John Press, 1978.

Overnight to Many Distant Cities. New York: G. P. Putnam's Sons, 1983. Includes: "They called for more structure . . . ," "Visitors," "Financially, the paper . . ." ["Pepperoni"], "Affection," "I put a name in an envelope . . . ," "Lightning," "That guy in the back room . . . ," "Captain Blood," "A woman seated on a plain wooden chair . . . ," "Conversations with Goethe," "Well we all had our Willie & Wade records . . . ," "Henrietta and Alexandra," "Speaking of the human body . . . ," "The Sea of Hesitation," "When he came . . ." ["The New Owner"], "Terminus," "The first thing the baby did wrong . . ." ["The Baby"], "The Mothball Fleet," "Now that I am older . . . ," "Wrack," "On our street . . ." ["Sakrete"], "The Palace at Four A.M.," "I am, at the moment . . . ," "Overnight to Many Distant Cities."

Sadness. New York: Farrar, Straus and Giroux, 1972. Includes: "Critique de la Vie Quotidienne," "Träumerei," "The Genius," "Perpetua," "A City of Churches," "The Party," "Engineer-Private Paul Klee Misplaces an Aircraft Between Milbertshofen and Cambrai, March 1916," "A Film," "The Sandman," "Departures," "Subpoena," "The Catechist," "The Flight of Pigeons from the Palace," "The Rise of Capitalism," "The Temptation of St. Anthony," "Daumier."

Sixty Stories. New York: G. P. Putnam's Sons, 1981. Includes stories from previous collections and these new titles: "Aria," "The Emerald," "How I Write My Songs," "The Farewell [Party]," "The Emperor," "Thailand," "Heroes," "Bishop," "Grandmother's House."

Unspeakable Practices, Unnatural Acts. New York: Farrar, Straus and Giroux, 1968. Includes: "The Indian Uprising," "The Balloon," "This Newspaper Here," "Robert Kennedy Saved from Drowning," "Report," "The Dolt," "The Police Band," "Edward and Pia," "A Few Moments of Sleeping and Waking," "Can We Talk," "Game," "Alice," "A Picture History of the War," "The President," "See the Moon?".

Uncollected Short Fiction

"Adventure." *Harper's Bazaar,* December 1970, 92–95.
"The Author." *New Yorker,* 15 June 1987, 27.
"Basil from Her Garden." *New Yorker,* 21 October 1985, 36–39. (Later published in *The Best American Short Stories 1986,* edited by Raymond Carver with Shannon Ravenel, 1–9. Boston: Houghton Mifflin, 1986.)
"The Bed." *Viva,* March 1974, 68–70.
"The Dassaud Prize." *New Yorker,* 12 January 1976, 26–29.
"Edwards, Amelia." *New Yorker,* 9 September 1972, 34–36.
"The Great Debate." *New Yorker,* 3 May 1976, 34–35.
"The Inauguration." *Harper's,* January 1973, 86–87.
"Kissing the President." *New Yorker,* 1 August 1983, 31.
"A Man." *New Yorker,* 30 December 1972, 26–27.
"Manfred" [with Karen Shaw]. *New York Times Magazine,* 18 April 1976, 87.
"Man's Face." *New Yorker,* 30 May 1964, 29.
"Monumental Folly" [with Edward Sorel]. *Atlantic,* February 1976, 33–40.
"Natural History." *Harper's,* August 1971, 44–45.
"Newsletter." *New Yorker,* 11 July 1970, 23.
"Philadelphia." *New Yorker,* 30 November 1968, 56–58.
"Presents." *Penthouse,* December 1977, 106–10.
"The Story Thus Far:" *New Yorker,* 1 May 1971, 42–45.
"Then." *Mother,* November–December 1964, 22–23.
"Three." *Fiction* 1, no. 1 (1972): 13.
"Tickets." *New Yorker,* 6 March 1989, 32–34.

Novels

The Dead Father. New York: Farrar, Straus and Giroux, 1975.
The King. New York: Harper and Row, 1990.
Paradise. New York: G. P. Putnam's Sons, 1986.
Snow White. New York: Atheneum, 1967.

Children's Book

The Slightly Irregular Fire Engine; or, The Hithering Thithering Djinn. New York: Farrar, Straus and Giroux, 1971.

Dramatic Adaptations

Great Days. Produced at American Place Theatre, New York, 8–26 June 1983.
Snow White. Rehearsed Reading. Produced at American Place Theatre, New York, 10 June 1976.

Picture-Text Collaboration

Sam's Bar: An American Landscape [with Seymour Chwast]. New York: Doubleday, 1987.

Nonfiction

"After Joyce." *Location* 1 (Summer 1964): 13–16.

"Culture, Etc." *Texas Observer*, 25 March 1960, 7.

"The Elegance Is Under Control." Review of *The Triumph*, by John Kenneth Galbraith. *New York Times Book Review*, 21 April 1968, 4–5.

"The Emerging Figure." University of Houston *Forum* 3 (Summer 1961): 23–24. (First published in Contemporary Arts Museum Catalogue, May–June 1961).

"The Most Wonderful Trick." *New York Times Book Review*, 25 November 1984, 3.

"Mr. Hunt's Wooly Utopia." Review of *Alpaca*, by H. L. Hunt. *Reporter*, 14 April 1960, 44–46.

"A Note on Elia Kazan." University of Houston *Forum* 1 (January 1957): 19–22.

"Not-Knowing." In *Voicelust*, edited by Alan Wier and Don Hendrie, Jr., 37–50. Lincoln: University of Nebraska Press, 1985. (Also published in *Georgia Review* 39 [Fall 1985]: 509–22; *The Pushcart Prize, 11: Best of the Small Presses*, edited by Bill Henderson, 23–27. Wainscott, N. Y.: Pushcart Press, 1986; and *The Best American Essays 1986*, edited by Elizabeth Hardwick, 9–24. New York: Ticknor and Fields, 1986.)

"The Tired Terror of Graham Greene." Review of *The Comedians*, by Graham Greene. *Holiday*, April 1966, 146, 148–49.

Untitled commentary on "Paraguay." In *Writer's Choice*, edited by Rust Hills, 25–26. New York: David McKay, 1974.

Secondary Work

Interviews and Sound Recordings

Baker, John F. "PW Interviews: Donald Barthelme." *Publishers Weekly*, 11 November 1974, 6–7.

Brans, Jo. "Embracing the World: An Interview with Donald Barthelme." *Southwest Review* 67 (Spring 1982): 121–37.

Donald Barthelme I, II, III, and IV. Pacifica Tape Library, BC2720.01–04, 1975.

Klinkowitz, Jerome. "Donald Barthelme." In *The New Fiction: Interviews with*

Innovative American Writers, edited by Joe David Bellamy, 45–54. Urbana: University of Illinois Press, 1974.

McCaffery, Larry. "An Interview with Donald Barthelme." In *Anything Can Happen: Interviews with Contemporary American Novelists*, edited by Tom LeClair and Larry McCaffery, 32–44. Urbana: University of Illinois Press, 1983.

O'Hara, J. D. "Donald Barthelme: The Art of Fiction LXVI." *Paris Review* 80 (Summer 1981): 181–210.

Schickel, Richard. "Freaked Out on Barthelme." *New York Times Magazine*, 16 August 1970, 14–15, 42.

"A Symposium on Fiction" [with Barthelme, William H. Gass, Grace Paley, and Walker Percy]. *Shenandoah* 27 (Winter 1976): 3–31.

Ziegler, Heide. "Donald Barthelme." In *The Radical Imagination and the Liberal Tradition: Interviews with English and American Novelists*, edited by Heide Ziegler and Christopher Bigsby, 39–59. London: Junction Books, 1982.

Books and Parts of Books

Bruss, Paul. "Barthelme's Short Stories: Ironic Suspensions of Text." In *Victims: Textual Strategies in Recent American Fiction*, 113–29. Lewisburg, Penn.: Bucknell University Press, 1981.

Couturier, Maurice, and Régis Durand. *Donald Barthelme*. New York and London: Methuen, 1982.

Durand, Régis. "On the Pertinaciousness of the Father, the Son, and the Subject: The Case of Donald Barthelme." In *Critical Angles: European Views of Contemporary American Literature*, edited by Marc Chénetier, 153–63. Carbondale: Southern Illinois University Press, 1986.

Gass, William H. "The Leading Edge of the Trash Phenomenon." In *Fiction and the Figures of Life*, 97–103. New York: Knopf, 1970. Rpt. from *The New York Review of Books*, 25 April 1968, 5–6.

Gilman, Richard. "Fiction: Donald Barthelme." In *The Confusion of Realms*, 42–52. New York: Random House, 1969.

Gordon, Lois. *Donald Barthelme*. Boston: Twayne, 1981.

Hassan, Ihab. *Paracriticisms*. Urbana: University of Illinois Press, 1975.

Hicks, Jack. "Metafiction and Donald Barthelme." In *In the Singer's Temple: Prose Fictions of Barthelme, Gaines, Brautigan, Piercy, Kesey, and Kosinski*, 18–82. Chapel Hill: University of N.C. Press, 1981.

Kazin, Alfred. *Bright Book of Life: American Novelists and Story Tellers from Hemingway to Mailer*. Boston: Little, Brown, 1973.

Klinkowitz, Jerome. *Literary Disruptions: The Making of a Post-Contemporary American Fiction*. Urbana: University of Illinois Press, 1975.

————. *The Self-Apparent Word: Fiction as Language/Language as Fiction.* Carbondale: Southern Illinois University Press, 1984.

McCaffery, Larry. "Donald Barthelme: The Aesthetics of Trash." In *The Metafictional Muse: The Works of Robert Coover, Donald Barthelme, and William H. Gass*, 99–150. Pittsburgh: University of Pittsburgh Press, 1982.

Molesworth, Charles. *Donald Barthelme's Fiction: The Ironist Saved from Drowning.* Columbia: University of Missouri Press, 1982.

Robison, James C. "1969–1980: Experiment and Tradition." In *The American Short Story, 1945–80: A Critical History*, edited by Gordon Weaver, 77–110. Boston: Twayne, 1983.

Stengel, Wayne B. *The Shape of Art in the Short Stories of Donald Barthelme.* Baton Rouge: Louisiana State University Press, 1985.

Tanner, Tony. *City of Words: American Fiction 1950–1970.* New York: Harper and Row, 1971.

Wilde, Alan. *Horizons of Assent: Modernism, Postmodernism, and the Ironic Imagination.* Baltimore: Johns Hopkins University Press, 1981.

————. *Middle Grounds: Studies in Contemporary American Fiction.* Philadelphia: University of Pennsylvania Press, 1987.

Zavarzadeh, Mas'ud. *The Mythopoeic Reality: The Postwar American Nonfiction Novel.* Urbana: University of Illinois Press, 1976.

Articles and Reviews

Aldridge, John W. "Dance of Death." *Atlantic Monthly,* July 1968, 89–91.

Barth, John. "The Literature of Exhaustion." *Atlantic Monthly,* August 1967, 29–34.

————. "Thinking Man's Minimalist: Honoring Barthelme," *New York Times Book Review,* 3 September 1989, 9.

Carver, Raymond. "Barthelme the Scribbler." Review of *Great Days. Texas Monthly,* March 1979, 162–63.

Chandra, Vikram [Sahaj]. "Good-bye, Mr. B." *Texas Monthly,* July 1990, 46–50.

Davis, Robert Murray. Review of *Overnight to Many Distant Cities. Studies in Short Fiction* 21 (Summer 1984): 277–79.

Dickstein, Morris. "Fantasy and Fable in Which Our Experimental Fiction Comes of Age." Review of *City Life. New York Times Book Review,* 26 April 1970, 1, 38–43.

————. "Fiction Hot and Kool: Dilemmas of the Experimental Writer." *TriQuarterly* 33 (Spring 1975): 257–72.

Ditsky, John M. "'With Ingenuity and Hard Work, Distracted': The Narrative Style of Donald Barthelme." *Style* 9 (Summer 1975): 388–400.

Donaghue, Denis. "For Brevity's Sake." Review of *Great Days. Saturday Review,* 3 March 1979, 50–52.

Evans, Walter. "Commanches and Civilization in Donald Barthelme's 'The Indian Uprising.'" *Arizona Quarterly* 42 (Spring 1986): 45–52.

Gass, William H. Untitled commentary. *Esquire*, August 1986, 46.

Gillen, Francis. "Donald Barthelme's City: A Guide." *Twentieth Century Literature* 18 (January 1972): 37–44.

James, Caryn. "Everything This Strange Is Real." Review of *Forty Stories. New York Times Book Review*, 25 October 1987, 14–15.

Johnson, Diane. "Possibly Parables." Review of *Great Days. New York Times Book Review*, 4 February 1979, 1, 36–37.

Johnson, R. E., Jr. "'Bees Barking in the Night': The End and Beginning of Donald Barthelme's Narrative." *Boundary 2*, 5 (Fall 1976): 71–92.

Leitch, Thomas M. "Donald Barthelme and the End of the End." *Modern Fiction Studies* 28 (Spring 1982): 129–43.

Leland, John. "Remarks Re-marked: Barthelme, What Curios of Signs!" *Boundary 2*, 5 (Spring 1977): 795–811.

Lingeman, Richard. "Steal My Name and You Got Trash." *New York Times Book Review*, 3 February 1974, 39.

Newman, Charles. "The Uses and Abuses of Death: A Little Rumble through the Remnants of Literary Culture." *TriQuarterly* 26 (Winter 1973): 3–41.

Oates, Joyce Carol. "Whose Side Are You On?" *New York Times Book Review*, 4 June 1972, 63.

Rother, James. "Parafiction: The Adjacent Universe of Barth, Barthelme, Pynchon, and Nabokov." *Boundary 2*, 5 (Fall 1976): 21–44.

Schmitz, Neil. "Donald Barthelme and the Emergence of Modern Satire." *Minnesota Review* 1 (Fall 1971): 109–18.

Scholes, Robert. "Metafiction." *Iowa Review* (Fall 1970): 100–115.

Shorris, Earl. "Donald Barthelme's Illustrated Wordy-Gurdy." *Harper's*, January 1973, 92–94, 96.

Stevick, Philip. "Lies, Fictions, and Mock Facts." *Western Humanities Review* 30 (Winter 1976): 1–12.

Stokes, Geoffrey. "Over Decades to Many Distant Cities." Review of *Overnight to Many Distant Cities. Village Voice*, 17 January 1984, 38–39.

Stott, William. "Donald Barthelme and the Death of Fiction." *Prospects* 1 (1975): 369–86.

Upton, Lee. "Failed Artists in Donald Barthelme's *Sixty Stories.*" *Critique* 26 (Fall 1984): 11–17.

Warde, William B., Jr. "Barthelme's 'The School.': Pedagogical Monologue and Social Commentary." *New Orleans Review* 8 (Summer 1981): 149–53.

———. "A Collage Approach: Donald Barthelme's Literary Fragments." *Journal of American Culture* 8 (Spring 1985): 51–56.

Whalen, Tom. "Wonderful Elegance: Barthelme's 'The Party.'" *Critique* 16 (1975): 44–48.

Bibliographies

Couturier, Maurice. "Barthelme, Donald." In *Postmodern Fiction: A Bio-Bibliographical Guide,* edited by Larry McCaffery, 260–63. Westport, Conn.: Greenwood Press, 1986.

Klinkowitz, Jerome, with Asa Pieratt and Robert Murray Davis. *Donald Barthelme: A Comprehensive Bibliography and Annotated Secondary Checklist.* Hamden, Conn.: Shoestring Press, 1977.

McCaffery, Larry. "Donald Barthelme, Robert Coover, William H. Gass: Three Checklists." *Bulletin of Bibliography* 31 (1974): 101–06.

Index

The Author

Barbara Roe teaches American literature, humanities, and twentieth-century interdisciplinary studies at Heritage Hall, a college-preparatory school in Oklahoma City, where she has been English Department chair since 1983. Under direction of Robert Murray Davis at the University of Oklahoma, she wrote her dissertation on Donald Barthelme's short fiction and received her Ph.D. in English in 1982. During her 14 years at Heritage Hall, she has received several honors for teaching excellence, including Distinguished Teacher, White House Scholars Program.

The Editor

Gordon Weaver earned his Ph.D. in English and creative writing at the University of Denver in 1970. He is professor of English at Oklahoma State University and serves as an adjunct member of the Vermont College Master of Fine Arts Writing Program. He is the author of several novels, including *Count a Lonely Cadence, Give Him a Stone, Circling Byzantium,* and most recently *The Eight Corners of the World* (1988). His short stories are collected in *The Entombed Man of Thule, Such Waltzing Was Not Easy, Getting Serious, Morality Play, A World Quite Round,* and *Men Who Would Be Good* (1991). Recognition of his fiction includes the St. Lawrence Award for Fiction (1973), two National Endowment for the Arts fellowships (1974 and 1989), and the O. Henry First Prize (1979). He edited *The American Short Story, 1945–1980: A Critical History* and is currently editor of *Cimarron Review.* Married and the father of three daughters, he lives in Stillwater, Oklahoma.